D0544857

THE
CURRY CLUB
FAVOURITE
RESTAURANT
CURRIES

Curry Club Books

250 Favourite Curries and Accompaniments
This latest bestseller is beautifully illustrated with colour
photographs and packed with new and exciting recipes and
traditional favourites

The Curry Club Balti Curry Cookbook
Over 100 easy-to-follow Balti recipes, including Balti restaurant
favourites and authenic recipes from Baltistan

The Curry Club Indian Restaurant Cookbook
Hints, tips and methods and approximately 150 recipes,
incorporating all your restaurant favourites

The Curry Club Indian Vegetarian Cookbook
150 totally new recipes, all vegetarian, all authentic to the Curry
Lands, plus helpful background information

The Curry Club Favourite Middle Eastern Recipes
150 spicy, tasty and delicious recipes from the 25 countries of the
Middle East plus plentiful background information

The Curry Club Chinese Restaurant Cookbook
Over 150 excellent recipes from top Chinese chefs and restaurants
around the world

The Little Curry Book
A perfect small gift, this book contains anecdotes, fables and
historical facts about curry, plus 16 popular recipes

The Good Curry Guide
A guide to the 1000 best curry restaurants in Britain

THE
CURRY CLUB
FAVOURITE
RESTAURANT
CURRIES

Pat Chapman

PIATKUS

Acknowledgement

The author and publisher are greatly indebted to B.E. International Ltd. for supplying the colour photographs of the dishes facing pages 65, 96, 129, 160. The dishes were all cooked by the author using their top quality Rajah brand spices.

© 1988 Pat Chapman

First published in 1988
by Judy Piatkus (Publishers) Limited
5 Windmill Street, London W1P 1HF

Reprinted 1989
Reprinted 1990 (twice)
Reprinted 1991
Reprinted 1992
Reprinted 1993

British Library Cataloguing in Publication Data
Chapman, Pat, *1940–*
The Curry Club favourite restaurant curries.
1. Food: Curried dishes. – Recipes.
I. Title
641.6'384

ISBN 0–86188–776–X
ISBN 0–86188–868–5 (Pbk)

Edited by Susan Fleming
Designed by Sue Ryall
Illustrated by Hanife Hassan O'Keeffe
Photography by John Lee

Phototypeset in 12 on 11.75 pt Lasercomp Palatino
Printed in Great Britain by Butler & Tanner Ltd, Frome and London

CONTENTS

INTRODUCTION

It is now well over five years since I wrote my first cookbook, *The Curry Club Indian Restaurant Cookbook*, and in that time a lot has happened. I have learnt many new techniques and recipes. The Curry Club is now in its seventh year, and the growth and interest in Indian food generally has mushroomed. Madhur Jaffrey's resoundingly successful TV series on Indian cooking has been repeated no less than five times; sales of 'ethnic' products shot up as a result, and even the big multiples took notice and began to stock them. Many new curry restaurants opened, bringing new ideas to the trade. Not only was red-flock wallpaper dispensed with in favour of light and airy furnishings and foliage, the standard heat-graded menu, with its choice of over a hundred curries, was also laid to rest by those restaurateurs who recognised a new awareness amongst their diners, in favour of a menu with a carefully selected choice of dishes.

Who could have predicted in 1948, when there were no more than six Indian restaurants in Britain, that 40 years on there would be 5,300? Over the last five years there have been 350 new openings a year and the trend shows no sign of deceleration – at almost one per day, that's a lot of curry houses!

Every year a number of market surveys are carried out for the catering industry measuring trends and spending levels. For the curry restaurateur, these reveal nothing but good news. In 1987, for example, it was estimated that for the first time the number of Indian restaurants exceeded Chinese. The surveys found curry was the nation's favourite dining-out food; that 2 million people ate restaurant curry each week, that they had an average age of 24, and that they visited a curry house twice a month. The surveys show a steady growth in first-time diners at curry restaurants, drawn not just from under 20-year-olds, but from all age groups, and they show that enjoyment of curry is not just a fad, it is here to stay.

Other surveys in the retail market provide similar statistics. The overall sale of spices and 'Indian related products' has grown from a trickle in the 1960s to a substantial amount. In 1987, around £25 million was spent in the retail sector on spices (with curry powder being the best seller). Multiples and specialist stores bulge with products that would have been unimaginable a few years ago. Fresh exotic fruit and vegetables are flown in every day, and the choice of spices, herbs and

basic exotic produce is nothing short of phenomenal. The British nation
has become hooked on curry.

My first book – *The Curry Club Indian Restaurant Cookbook* – has
done what it was intended to do. It contains most restaurant standard
recipes and shows how to produce them at home. It also includes recipes
which rarely appear in restaurants but which show useful techniques
designed both to encourage the cook to do new things and to show
the correct use of spicing. All of this information – the 150 recipes, with
the 30-page techniques introduction – is basic and essential.

However, in the five years since I wrote it, I've learned a lot more
from the restaurants. Indeed, I've had the privilege of working in Indian
restaurant kitchens in Delhi and Bombay as well as some in London,
working alongside the professionals. I want to share their 'secrets' with
you. What better way than by inviting the professionals to contribute
recipes to the book. The selection of restaurants involved quite a lot of
research. Armed with *The Good Curry Guide*, I made a short list of 200
restaurants, all the best in their particular field. I acquired their menus,
then selected one or two particular dishes which looked interesting or
special. That way I was able to select the widest possible range of
recipes and there would be no repetition.

I was sure that some would not wish to give away their 'secrets'. I
was quite wrong, of course, as nearly all responded with promptness,
generosity and sincerity, with carefully written recipes and enthusiastic
approval and good wishes for my project. For the next few weeks,
opening the post was really exciting. Reading the work of such experts
was indeed a mouthwatering task – as I'm sure you'll agree when you
flip through these pages. Next came the task of selecting which recipes
to use, and of re-writing them so that they would appear in uniform
format. At the same time I tested them to prove that they actually
worked. I have done this because it is a very different matter cooking
for 20, 50 or 100 and more, to cooking small portions at home. As far
as 'secrets' are concerned, it is my belief that the better quality the
restaurant, the less 'secrets' they have. The owner or chef of a really
good restaurant is not going to be frightened of losing custom because
he gives away recipes. If his cooking is good, he will always be assured
of clientele, indeed the diner who succeeds in cooking a particular dish
at home will return to that restaurant with greater appreciation and
understanding of the skills required by the restaurant chef.

Some of the recipes came from restaurants and chefs continents away.
A good number came from the sub-continent itself – others from curry
restaurants as far apart as Australia, Los Angeles, New York and Nairobi.
Most are favourite restaurants within the British Isles.

I am most grateful to owners and chefs, to the management and staff
of all the restaurants involved and hope they enjoy seeing their recipes
in print. Above all I hope that you will enjoy trying out these recipes

and hopefully learning new and exciting techniques and expanding your curry cooking repertoire to match those of the very best restaurants in the world.

I hope your favourite dish is here, but if it doesn't appear in either book forgive me please. For I quickly found that it would have been very easy to have added another 150 recipes for first-class speciality dishes from another 150 restaurants of equal quality – enough for another book. But we'll just have to save these recipes until next time.

Pat Chapman
The Curry Club, Haslemere,
March 1988

THE RESTAURANTS

Afghan Buzkash,
    London SW15
Agra, Warminster
Air India
Ameena, Birmingham
Asha, Liverpool
Ashoka, Belfast
Asia, Salisbury

Balaka, Hull
Beewees, London N4
Bekash, Milton Keynes
Bengal Lancer,
    London NW5
Blue Elephant,
    London SW6
Bombay, Norwich
Bombay Brasserie,
    London SW7
British Raj, Royston
Bukharra, Delhi

Chesham Tandoori,
    Chesham
Curry Fever, Leicester

Days of The Raj,
    Birmingham
Deansgate Tandoori,
    Manchester
Dewanian, London
    SE23
Dilruba, Rugby
Dilshad, Cleveland
Dilshad,
    Wolverhampton

Everest, Cardiff

Fisherman's Cove,
    Madras
Fort Aguada, Goa
Friends Corner,
    Coventry

Ganges, Exeter,
    Plymouth, Torbay,
    Truro
Ganges, Bristol
Gaylord, London W1
Grand Indian, Bedford
Green Bengal,
    Birmingham

India, Folkestone
Indian Railways
Indus Curry,
    Colchester

Jamundi, London WC2
Johni Gurkas,
    Aldershot
Jhorna, Orpington

Kalpna, Edinburgh
Kathmandu,
    Manchester

Kensington Tandoori, London W8
Khyber, Plymouth
Kohinoor, Preston
Koh-i-noor, Newport, Gwent
Kuti's, Southampton

Laguna, Leicester
Lake Palace, Udaipur
Lal Quilla, Liphook
Lancers, Edinburgh
Last Days of the Raj, London WC2
Light of India, Ilford
Light of India, Jersey

Madhu's Brilliant, Southall
Magna, Bedford
Malabar, London W8
Mandalay, Leeds
Mandalay, London SE10
Mandeer, London W1
Manzil, Birkenhead
Miah's, Edinburgh
Mogul-e-Azam, Nottingham
Mughal Sheraton, Agra
Mumtaz, Peterborough
Munbhave, Croydon

Nawab, Harrow

Nirmal's, Sheffield

Oakham Tandoori, Leicester
Oberoi Intercontinental, Delhi

Palace Tandoori, London W6
Palash, Portsmouth
Parveen, London N1
Polash, Shoeburyness

Raffles, Singapore
Raj Leith, Edinburgh
Raj Belash, Cambridge
Raj Tandoori, London EC1
Rajdoot, Birmingham, Bristol, Manchester, Dublin
Rajpoot, Bath
Red Fort, London W1
Rong Mahal, Adelaide
Romna Gate, London N14
Rupali, Newcastle

Safeer, Nairobi
Salloo's, London SW1
Shalimar, Perth
Sheik's, Bradford
Shish Mahal, Aberdeen
Shish Mahal, Glasgow
Simla, Haslemere

Simla, Llangollen and Oswestry
Sonar Gaon, London N1
Star of Asia, Oxford
Sultan, Chipping Sodbury
Surma, Ely

Taj Mahal, Chelmsford
Taj Mahal Intercontinental, Bombay
Taj Mahal, Leigh
Taj Mahal, Oxford
Taj Mahal, Penzance and Falmouth
Taj Samundra, Sri Lanka
Tandoori Oven, Bournemouth
Tea Planters' Tiffin House, Hove
Tithas, Camberley

Veeraswamy, London W1
Verandah, Edinburgh
Viceroy of India, Biggleswade, Bedfordshire
Viceroy of India, London NW1
Viceroy of India, Swansea

1
USEFUL INFORMATION

For two reasons I have decided to start this chapter in a slightly unusual way for a cookbook – by describing the daily routine at the average curry house. It is not that these routines have much, if anything, in common with our own household routines – nor with those of the household in India. Nor do I include this information to assist those whose ambition it is to open their own restaurant.

The first reason for including it is that it is fascinating to understand how an establishment copes with providing, almost instantly, the many dishes on its menu. The second is that there are certain methods and techniques which we can use to advantage in our own cooking.

The remainder of this chapter contains other useful background information, which you need to understand in order to produce curry dishes.

The Curry House Routine

Running a curry restaurant is a complicated business, requiring a number of skills. Most curry houses do a small lunch trade (although many do well at Sunday lunchtime) and busy evenings – Saturday is the busiest and Monday the quietest. The average 80-seater can easily serve 200 diners on Saturday, but only 30 on Monday. It will serve 700 people in a week.

Recently I was privileged enough to be invited to 'guest chef' at both The Bengal Lancer, 253 Kentish Town Road, London NW5 and The North West Frontier, 310 Caledonian Road, London N1 for four days each. It was a fascinating experience. I observed the daily routine in these two restaurants, and it is no doubt identical in most of the 5,300 curry establishments up and down the country.

At 10 am the kitchen staff assembles and it does its preparation for the day. A medium sized curry house has a kitchen brigade of six for each 100 seats. One will be on holiday or on his day off. The others all have specific jobs to do. Two will prepare the garlic, onions and vegetables and top up their curry gravy. One will butcher the meat, preparing 25–50 lb (11–22 kg) of leg meat, depending on how busy they expect to be (i.e. which day of the week it is). Another will prepare chickens, skinning, boning and dicing them. The fifth man will be making tandoori marinades, firing up the clay oven, making bread dough and washing the rice. By midday most of the preparation is done and cauldrons are simmering on the stove. Mutton is being mildly curried, so is chicken and a lentil dish. Another huge pot is bubbling away with curry masala gravy.

The vegetable man delivers a sack of onions, 6 lb (2.7 kg) of garlic, and a huge assortment of vegetables. It is quickly chopped up. There is already a mountain of garlic – not chopped, just peeled – and a huge bucket full of peeled onions. The buckets are topped up. Deftly and very fast vegetables are got ready for onion salad, mushroom bhajee and so on. Some of the mutton is placed in a bucket of vivid orange marinade, whilst chicken quarters and breast cubes are placed in plastic buckets containing red marinade. 'For tikka and tandoori,' grunts the tandoor chef, at the same time prodding the charcoal at the bottom of his clay oven.

In the restaurant five of the six waiters are at work cleaning, polishing, laying up tables, re-stocking the bar and re-ordering drink from their supplier.

Then it's lunchtime. About twelve people come in between 12.30 and 2 and they are served.

Meanwhile the kitchen is still hard at work preparing for the evening. By now the meat has cooked; it is completely tender and has been strained and allowed to cool. Amazingly they throw away the lovely stock juices. It's the same with the chicken and the vegetables.

At around 2 o'clock, someone half-cooks two huge saucepans of rice – one plain boiled, the other pullao rice. Once both are ready they are put into a warm oven. This will finish off the grains slowly, allow them to become separate, and will be perfect for the evening.

At 3 o'clock everything is ready and they all take a three-hour break.

Six-thirty and everything is humming. The first customers have placed their orders. The waiter takes his written slips to the kitchen. The tandoor chef loads up his 4 foot (1.2 metre) long skewers and places his kebabs and tikkas into the white hot coals. He grabs a tennis-ball-sized piece of dough and, as he deftly slaps it between his hands, it becomes a naan. He carefully places it on a rounded pad covered with a teatowel and with this he places the naan on to the inside wall of the tandoor to which it sticks and elongates into its familiar tear-shape whilst cooking. At the stove two chefs take long-handled frying pans in which they heat some ghee over the high-pressure gas stove. Then they add this and that spice from an array of plastic tubs in front of them. A flick of a giant cooking spoon and in goes a dollop of curry gravy. The pan is clattered back and forth and intentionally made to flambé. A huge sheet of flame whoofs up and at once dies – it caramelises the spices in the pan, I'm told. In go the cooked meat and cream and almonds for a korma. In another pan it's chicken dhansak: lentils and other vegetables are made to flare then simmer. The pans seem to burst into life all at once. The cooked food is then put into warm serving dishes, along with the rice, and taken off by the waiters.

By 7.30 the restaurant is full: 80 people are being served. The kitchen is going full tilt. The two huge stoves are always in use, as is the tandoor. The washer-up is equally busy, and for the five kitchen staff and five waiters work goes on without a break for another $5\frac{1}{2}$ hours until the restaurant shuts at 1 am. Some 200 people have ordered up to 1,000 items between them. Everything went smoothly tonight – it usually does. The staff finally relax and eat their own meal – a mutton and chick pea curry they cooked for themselves during the bedlam. Little is said as they scoop up their meal with chupattis. But there is hardly any food left over, and there is still the kitchen to clean up. By 2 am the last of them has locked up and gone home to a well-earned bed, safe in the knowledge that the same routine will start up again at 10 am in the morning. Who ever said catering was easy?

Kitchen Equipment

In the recipes which follow, you will need a frying pan, a grill pan and wire rack, two or three saucepans, the largest of which should be 5 pints (3 litres), about 8 inches (20 cm) in diameter and 5 inches (13 cm) deep. You will also need one or more lidded casserole dishes of between $3\frac{1}{2}$– 5 pints (2–3 litres) capacity, and ordinary oven baking trays. For preparation work you need large and small mixing bowls, measuring equipment, sharp knives and a rolling pin and board. The average kitchen should already have all this equipment.

Two special Indian cooking pans which I find extremely useful are the *karahi* or *kadahi* and the *tawa* or *tava*. The karahi is the Indian version of the Chinese wok. Traditionally it is made of cast iron, has two handles and a rounded bottom for use over charcoal fires. Modern karahis are made from pressed carbon steel and the bottom is flattened to enable the pan to be used on modern stoves. The karahi is an all-purpose cooking pan used for stir-frying, simmering, frying and deep-frying. Its hemispherical shape makes it efficient in a way that a conventional frying pan or saucepan is not. The heat is at its hottest on the flat part and it then gets progressively cooler the higher up the sides you go. This enables the cook to control the temperature of the ingredients by shifting them from the centre outwards. The shape of the karahi makes it very efficient for deep-frying. A conventional saucepan, being flat bottomed with straight sides, requires more oil than the curved-sided karahi. Both of these pans are worth investing in. They can be obtained by mail order from The Curry Club, see Appendix 1.

Ever since Kenwood invented their Kenwood Chef, the cook's life has been made easy. Jobs such as making purées and doughs, shredding, slicing, peeling and grinding, became virtually instant and absolutely effortless. Blenders and liquidisers are ideal for making purées.

The new-style food processor purées just about anything, without liquid, and is particularly good for garlic, ginger and onion. I also find it perfect for 'grinding' meat for kebabs. It achieves the fine pounded texture akin to the authentic stone-pounded technique, especially when fresh garlic, ginger, coriander, chilli and spices are thrown in too. The difference is that the processor does in 60 seconds what the Indian villager would need 60 minutes' hard labour to do.

Other useful tools include thermostatically controlled deep-fryers, slow cookers (excellent for curry making in place of casseroling), rice cookers (again excellent, but expensive if seldom used) and yoghurt makers.

Electric coffee grinders manage to grind most spices in small doses, but a newly developed product by Kenwood – the spice mill designed to fit on to the Kenwood Chef – does a much better job. Every serious curry cook should invest in one.

Spices

Spices are vegetable matter: most are seeds, pods or berries, while others are dry leaves, stigma, buds, roots, rhizomes, even resin. They are harvested from trees, shrubs, plants or flowers.

Most spices taken on their own are bitter, unpalatable and in some cases inedible (cassia or cinnamon bark for example), but used correctly in small amounts, singly, or in combination, they add flavour to food. There are over 60 whole spices that can be used in Indian cooking. Fortunately some of these are rarely used, whilst some are virtually indispensible. Some are used whole, some ground. The questions which face the curry cook are what spices to purchase, in what quantities, where can they be obtained, how much will they cost, and how long will they last. I have listed all the spices used in this book in Appendix 2, along with sensible storage quantities.

As to the cost, even if one bought everything listed in Appendix 2, the total is minimal – certainly no more than the cost of one good meal at a restaurant, and of course the enjoyment of using the spices more than offsets its small cost in terms of money. Frequency of usage depends on how often you decide to cook a curry!

STORING SPICES

Whole spices retain their flavour longer than ground, for one year or more sometimes. Ground spices give off a stronger aroma than whole, and of course this means their storage life is that much shorter. Three months is about right for most ground items. So plan your larder accordingly, and buy little and often and grind freshly. Keep the spices out of sunlight (better in a dark pantry) and in airtight labelled containers. Coffee or jam jars are excellent.

GRINDING SPICES

It is better by far to grind your own whole spices whenever you can. Firstly you can be sure of the quality and contents, and secondly they will be fresher and tastier. The traditional method is by mortar and pestle, but you can use an electric coffee grinder or the new Kenwood spice mill. After a damp wipe a coffee grinder can still be used for coffee – it might even enhance the flavour! Use small quantities to prevent overloading the motor.

Don't try to grind dry ginger or turmeric. They are too fibrous for most small grinders, and commercial powders are adequate. Peppers – chilli, paprika and black or white pepper – are tricky, and commercially ground powders will suffice. The oilier spices such as cloves, nutmeg, brown cardamoms and bay leaves are easier to grind if roasted first.

In the recipes, when a spice if referred to as 'ground', this means factory ground. Where it requires the spice to be home ground (usually after roasting), the recipe clearly states this.

ROASTING SPICES

Whole spices are roasted to enhance or change the flavour. The process is simple and can be done in a dry pan on the stove, in a dry electric frying pan, under the grill or in the oven. Each spice should be heated until it gives off an aroma. The heat should be medium rather than hot and the time required is a few minutes. The spice should not blacken, a light brown at most is sufficient. The original oil of the spice must not be totally cooked out or it will lose its flavour. A little experimenting will soon show you how to do it. In some recipes pre-roasted spices are important (see garam masala, pages 42–3).

Herbs

The use of herbs in cooking performs a similar function to spices – to add flavour to food. They are usually fresh or dried leaves of plants cultivated exclusively for the purpose. They also add greatly to the appearance of a dish when used as garnishes. The use of herbs is, of course, widespread in Mediterranean countries such as France, Italy and Greece. Middle Eastern cooking uses almost as many spices as Indian, but it also uses a wide selection of herbs. Considering the historical relationship between the Arabs and India in terms of trade and invasions over the last 2,000–3,000 years, it is surprising that the use of herbs in Indian cooking is minimal. In fact, the main herb is fresh coriander leaf which has a very distinctive, acquired, musky taste, a little redolent of the not unpleasant fragrance of candle wax. But it is a very important taste which contributes greatly to achieving both 'that restaurant taste' and authentic flavours.

The other herb which is used from time to time is mint, particularly spearmint. Its use will crop up in a few of the recipes which follow. A tiny pinch of dried mint livens up many curry dishes, giving them a fresh taste. Add it 10 minutes before the end of cooking.

SELECTED CURRY INGREDIENTS

Certain ingredients are used to add texture and/or flavour to Indian cooking, chief of which are garlic, ginger and onion (see Chapter 2), coconut, chilli, oils and dairy products.

COCONUT

Coconut is used extensively in South India and Bengal and all the curry lands to the East. Desiccated coconut is one substitute for fresh coconut and can be used by adding it dry to your cooking, or by simmering it in water and straining it to create coconut 'milk'. A new product to this country is coconut powder – very finely ground dry coconut flesh – which has a creamier taste than desiccated, and mixes well with water.

To choose a fresh coconut, shake before buying to ensure it is full of liquid (the more liquid it has the fresher it is). Coconuts without liquid or with mouldy or wet eyes should not be used.

To use:

1 Make a hole in two of the three eyes with a screwdriver or nail. Drain off and keep the liquid (coconut water).
2 Bake empty coconut in oven at 400°F/200°C/Gas 6 for 15 minutes.
3 While still hot crack it with a hammer. Remove the flesh.
4 Cut into 1 inch (2.5 cm) cubes and soak in water for 4 hours.
5 Strain the flesh, keeping the liquid.
6 Squeeze the flesh to get remaining liquid.
7 Combine the liquids from 1, 5 and 6 to make coconut milk.

Use the flesh, in chunks or puréed in curries.

The familiar 7 oz (200 g) rich block of 'creamed coconut' is a combination of freshly grated coconut flesh and coconut oil, which sets solid. To use this boil a little water. Cut off the amount required and melt it in the hot water. If you try to fry it without water, it will burn. It must be kept under refrigeration.

Coconut oil comes set solid in bottles with no instructions as to how to extract it. It is, however, simple. Ensure the cap is screwed on tightly then immerse the bottle in hot water for a few minutes. The oil becomes transparent as it melts.

CHILLI, PEPPER AND HEAT

Chilli peppers, of which there are over 1,500 species, are native to Mexico and the tropical forests of Central and Southern America. They were not discovered until the fifteenth century when Spanish and

Portuguese explorers stumbled across them, along with tobacco, the potato, the tomato, the turkey and sweetcorn. It did not take long for the chilli to be carried across oceans to India. The Portuguese took them to their southern Indian bases, and the southern Indians took to chillies like ducks to water. Up until that time, and for thousands of years before, black peppercorn had been the 'heat' agent; indeed it remains India's greatest export – the 'King of Spices' – to this day.

Pepper and chilli have one factor in common – they create a burning sensation in the mouth. This causes the brain to activate the salivary glands to 'wash away' the irritant. The nose runs and the body perspires. Researchers believe this is one reason why chillies are popular in hot countries – they claim that chillies actually cool you down. They also believe that the high level of the alkaloid capsaicin – the measure of 'heat' in food – which is present in peppers is the reason why chilli in particular and curry in general is mildly addictive. Capsaicin is related to caffeine, nicotine and morphine. I for one enjoy 'hot' food and I get withdrawal symptoms if I have to abstain from my curry for more than a couple of weeks.... I just have to take a fix! But the scientists assure us that this addiction is very slight and quite harmless.

OILS AND GHEE

Curry cooking depends very greatly on the use of oil to establish both taste and texture, particularly in the early stages of cooking. And there is no argument that using *more* oil creates a better curry than using less. There is a limit to this, of course. We are all probably familiar with curries served at restaurants swimming in oil. In such a case, too much oil was used in the first place, and no matter how good the end result, the excess oil spoils the dish. It could so easily have been spooned off at the end of its cooking while still in its saucepan. Once a properly cooked curry is taken off direct heat and allowed to rest, all the oil rises to the top and can then be ladled off for future use in curry cooking.

These days nutritionists are aware of health risks concerning certain fats and oils. Solid fats are described as saturated and can lead to a build-up of cholesterol in the body. Saturated fats include rendered animal fat such as dripping and lard. Butter, clarified butter and butter ghee are in this category and to a lesser extent solid margarine and vegetable ghee. Ghee is widely used in the cooking of northern India and its neighbours.

Oils are extensively used in southern India. Those described as poly-unsaturated are said to be better and these include certain vegetable oils such as sunflower and soya oil. Best of all are said to be mono-unsaturated oils which include peanut, mustard blend and olive oil. The first two are excellent for curry cooking, but olive oil has too strong a flavour.

In many dishes the oil used affects the final taste very minimally, so most oils can be used instead of ghee. But in rice and bread cooking, ghee imparts an important flavour. I have tried to strike a happy balance in these recipes by specifying neither too much nor too little ghee or oil. You can always use more if that is to your taste, and remember to spoon off excess before serving.

DAIRY ITEMS

Indians are great milk consumers. They use the milk of cows, buffalo and goats. They make cream and yoghurt, but cheese isn't traditional. Indian cheese (paneer) is a simple form of cottage cheese, actually the curds separated from the whey (page 41). The whey can be used as vegetable stock or in soups.

Yoghurt is easy to make at home. Yoghurt is ordinary milk (not UHT) which has been fermented by means of heat and a starter bacteria (usually other yoghurt).

Condensed milk (koya) is used in Indian sweets and is made by continually stirring milk until it reduces to a thick texture. Powdered milk can be used in certain recipes in place of cream or koya. In every curry house you'll see a huge saucepan in a warm place in which the day's yoghurt is made.

Some Indian restaurant chefs use ordinary milk as a cooking ingredient in curry. It reduces to a nice thick gravy, and when it is added to curries with slightly acidic ingredients (tomatoes or vinegar, for example) the milk can 'curdle', i.e. turn into curds and whey, but this is not an unpleasant effect; the curds are minute and virtually tasteless.

Evaporated milk can be used to obtain a creamy taste in kormas, etc.

CHEMICALS IN FOOD

Spices are used in Indian cookery primarily to enhance the taste of the principal ingredients. They also affect the colour of the dish. Turmeric is used to give yellows; coriander, cummin, clove, etc for shades of brown; paprika and chilli powder for red; fresh coriander and chilli for green. Saffron, the world's most expensive spice, gives a bright orangey-gold colour, and deep crimson is obtained by use of *ratan jot* (similar to alkenet root). Natural colours such as these have been used in the sub-continent for as long as anyone can remember.

It took the latter half of the twentieth century and food factories to forget the old ways. In the interests of time and cost saving, chemicals have crept into so many Western food products that I haven't space to mention them. Not surprisingly, chemical technology has crept into Indian food as well.

Nowhere is this more apparent than in the tandoori/tikka department. Those bright orangey-red chunks of chicken and lamb look so attractive on their beds of lettuce, onion rings and lemon wedges, but it's all, quite frankly, baloney. The authentic dish in the Punjab, from where this style of cooking originated, looks pale and anaemic in its natural un-dyed state but is, of course, just as tasty, for these chemicals are quite tasteless.

I am not emotive about the use of chemical colourants in food. I am not allergic to them, but like everyone else, including the manufacturers, I don't know what, if any, their cumulative effect is. I listen to the contemporary debate and I feel the manufacturers should listen too. My conclusion is that when I cook for the public I must do without chemicals, so I set about looking for alternatives. I found a substitute for the deep red colour in beetroot powder and for yellow in annatto seed powder. Combinations of these work well for tandoori. The colourful pullao rice at the restaurants makes use of a sunset yellow chemical. What should be used is saffron, which gives a delightful orange yellow colour *plus* the bonus of fragrance, but its cost prohibits most restaurants from using it. Other chemicals used on rice include red, orange and green. Restaurant rice is particularly attractive and for those who wish to copy it I give the colouring method in the chapter on rice and bread.

KEEPING CURRIES

I find two schools of thought about curry. One is that it should be cooked and served 'fresh', the other that it is better left for a day or two to marinate. Neither restaurants nor cooks in the Indian home would leave a completely cooked curry overnight. In the restaurant it could lead to quality control and health problems, and it's not the way they cook the dishes anyway. In India, without adequate refrigeration, the ambient temperature would cause the food to go off within hours.

But given a refrigerator and sensible quality control, keeping a fresh curry overnight is safe enough. Provided that the raw ingredients are absolutely fresh, not frozen, and are cooked immediately, and provided that the dish is cooled rapidly after cooking, covered and placed in the fridge at once, then it will be safe for up to 48 hours. It will change in both taste and texture. One school of thought prefers it this way. It will be better marinated, but this usually means the spices will become blander and the principal ingredient softer. If you prefer this method of preparation, I would suggest you observe the following points:

1 Do not keep fish or shellfish curries in this way.
2 If you intend to keep a curry for a day or two, undercook it slightly, i.e. cut back the timings by 10 minutes. You will obtain a better texture when re-heating — simply simmer until perfectly ready.
3 Use common sense about which vegetables will keep.
4 Inspect meat or chicken after 24 hours. Smell and taste it. It should look firm and good.
5 Ensure that the curry is reheated — simmered — for at least 10 minutes.
6 During reheating, taste, and if it needs a boost of a little more spicing, add early so that they cook in well.

FREEZING CURRIES

Curries freeze as well as any other dish. Here are a few observations.

1 Use only fresh ingredients, not items that have come from the freezer.
2 Choose your subject carefully. Some ingredients are not suitable for freezing — their texture is unpleasant when thawed, for instance. Meat and poultry are excellent, as are all lentil dishes. Some vegetables work well — aubergines, peas, beans, carrots — while others don't — potato, okra, marrow, etc. Fish and seafood work well. Rice is satisfactory but I can never see the point — it takes less time to make fresh rice (and it has better taste and texture).
3 Always undercook a dish destined for the freezer by about 10 minutes to allow for 'tenderising' in the freezing process and reheating.
4 Take out any large whole spices before freezing, especially cassia, cardamoms and cloves as they tend to go a bit astringent.
5 Get the dish into the freezer as soon as you can once it is cool.
6 Be aware that spicy food can 'taint' other foods, so preferably pack in a plastic container with an airtight lid.
7 Label contents and freeze date.
8 Use within 3 months.
9 When reheating ensure that the dish is thoroughly hot and cooked through.
10 You may find the spicing has gone a little bland, so taste and add more spices as needed.

2
CURRY BASES & BASICS

In my view, this chapter is the most important in the book to the cook aiming to capture that restaurant taste. Here you will find recipes which deal specifically with the cooking of spices and curry bases. These recipes are referred to throughout the book.

You can make the same curry in a number of different ways. For example, you may wish to use a mixture of dry spices (such as the following curry powder) made into a paste and fried, or you may wish to use a pre-made paste. You might prefer to use garlic, ginger or onion purée on one occasion, whereas you might like to chop them and fry them unpuréed on another. Alternatively you might choose to use the curry masala gravy technique from page 30. You will find that you can use alternative 'base' methods from this chapter at the initial cooking stages to achieve the same end result. It is impractical to state this in all the recipes — it would take up too much space — but I do hope you will simply use the recipes as a guide, either following them precisely, or taking an alternative 'route', using shortcuts or making changes as the mood takes you.

Whichever way you set about cooking curry, remember that the most important factor is to maintain a correct texture — thick and creamy. Maintaining a good balance between oil and water is the key to obtaining the restaurant-style dish. Apart from that observation, there is no reason at all why you should not be completely flexible in your approach.

CURRY TECHNIQUES

There are several ways of utilising the spices and flavourings for curry making, and it is necessary to outline these before we begin.

The first 'stage' is the mixing together of the ground spices, the masala — the unique combination which makes Indian style cooking so distinctive. The following curry powder recipe is a masala, but throughout the recipes I refer to the masala as **Spices** (whole or ground).

As the spices need to be cooked slightly to get rid of raw tastes, the next step is to make them into a paste with a little water. The cooking can be done by simply adding the powder to hot oil (many restaurant cooks do this), but it is very easy to burn the spices this way, and a paste is safer. The cooking of the masala — the bhoona — is the next stage.

The cooking of whole spices as opposed to ground — the bargar — is another technique which I outline, as is the puréeing and cooking of onion, ginger, garlic and coriander.

Mild curry powder

Commercial curry powder has two drawbacks in my view. Firstly, although the manufacturers are supposed to list the ingredients, some avoid it by simply stating 'spices'; and even if they do list them, they do not state the quantities. They often put in too much chilli, salt and, in some cases, chemical colourings and preservatives. Undeclared additives can include husks and stalks and other adulterations.

The second drawback is that the use of the same curry powder blend in all the recipes would make each dish taste virtually the same.

However, it is sometimes useful to have curry powder in the larder. You can purchase a commercial version or you can make up your own with this interesting mixture. It comes from the first cookery book given to a young bride who, with her husband, was posted to the British army base in Agra in 1904. The lady was my grandmother and that book was her bible. It was first published in 1870, so this curry powder has been recipe tested for 120 years, in itself an amazing fact.

The following recipe will give you around 9 oz (250 g) of curry powder.

A heaped teaspoon is about 5 g on average. It's not easy to transpose to Imperial.

60 g coriander seeds

30 g white cummin seeds

20 g fenugreek seeds

25 g gram flour (besan)

25 g garlic powder

20 g paprika

20 g turmeric

20 g aromatic garam masala

5 g dry ground curry
  leaves

5 g asafoetida

5 g ginger powder

5 g chilli powder

5 g yellow mustard powder

5 g ground black pepper

1 Roast and then grind the first three spices.
2 Mix all together well and store.
3 Omit the final four spices for a totally mild curry powder.
4 For those who wish, salt and sugar (white granulated) can be added during the blending: add 2 tablespoons sugar and/or 1 teaspoon salt.

To make a dish for four you would need about 1 oz (25 g) of curry powder, so this will give you 10 portions. I prefer to make a reasonable batch like 9 oz (250 g) because it 'matures' or becomes better blended the longer it is stored. It can be used at once, of course, but after about a month it is perfect. Do not keep it for longer than 18 months — it tends to lose its subtle flavours, becoming bitter. Store in an airtight container in a dark damp-free place.

THE MASALA PASTE

When a recipe states 'mix and blend dry spices' (a masala), such as in the previous curry powder mixture, it is necessary to cook those spices to remove the raw tastes. This is most safely done by making up a paste with water to obtain a thickish texture. The water prevents the spices from burning up when they are introduced to the oil in the bhoona or frying process.

1 Select a mixing bowl large enough to enable you to stir the masala.
2 Stir the masala until it is fully mixed.
3 Add enough water *and no more* to form a stiff paste.
4 Leave to stand for a minimum of 10 minutes. It does not matter how *long* it stands. This ensures that the ground spices absorb all the water.
5 Add a little water if it is too dry prior to using in the bhoona or frying process.

THE BHOONA

The bhoona is the Hindi term for the process of cooking the spice paste in hot oil. This is an important part of the curry cooking process which removes the raw taste of the spices and influences the final taste of the dish. Use the bhoona method whenever the recipes in this book state that you should 'fry the spices'. In fact, traditionally you should fry the spice paste first then add the puréed or chopped onion second. This method can easily cause burned spices so I reverse this process and I have found that it works very satisfactorily.

1 Take a round-sided pan such as a karahi or wok. If you don't have one, use an ordinary frying pan (a non-stick one is best).

2 Heat the oil to quite a high heat (but not smoking).

3 Remove the pan from the heat and at once gently add the onion purée. Return to the heat and commence stirring.

4 *From this point do not let your attention wander.* Keep stirring the purée until the oil is hot again then gently add the masala paste. Beware of splattering.

5 Keep stirring. The water in the paste lowers the temperature. Do not let the mixture stick at all. Do not stop stirring, not even for a few seconds.

6 After a few minutes the water will have evaporated out and the oil will float above the mixture. The spices will be cooked. Remove the pan from the heat. Proceed with the remainder of the recipe.

THE BARGAR

Some of the recipes in this book require you to fry whole *spices. The process is for the same reason as the bhoona — to cook out the raw taste from the spices. Again the oil should be hot, and the spices are put into the oil with no water or purée. You must use your judgement as to when they are cooked. Do not let them blacken. As soon as they begin to change colour or to float they are ready. It will not take more than a couple of minutes.*

If you do burn the bhoona or bargar process you must throw the result away and start again. Better to waste a small amount of spices than taint a whole meal.

THE PURÉE

The importance of the purée cannot be overstated, and it is the way the restaurants achieve that gorgeous creamy texture. It is based on tradition, of course. In the Indian home the purée is made the hard way by wet-grinding spices with garlic and/or ginger and/or onion to a fine texture, and it is time-consuming and messy. We are fortunate to have electric blenders and food processors to do the job in seconds. I have heard a purist school of thought which says that metal blades taint the items being ground, but every restaurant uses this method and it doesn't seem to taint their dishes.

I have given large quantities for each of these purées as it saves time, smells and washing up to make large batches then freeze the surplus in ice-cube moulds or empty yoghurt tubs.

GARLIC PURÉE

Real garlic is best and many curry restaurants use it. I still use garlic powder from time to time but it contains flour and gives a distinctive flavour. An expensive (but good) product is garlic purée in tubes. A product I have used a lot recently (as do many restaurants) is dehydrated garlic flakes: to use, soak in an equal volume of water for 30 minutes then mulch down in a food processor or blender. The taste is nearly as good as the real (fresh) thing, and the texture is indistinguishable.

One plump clove of garlic is the equivalent of 1 level teaspoon garlic purée. An ice cube container holds 3 teaspoons of purée.

**30 plump garlic cloves,
    peeled**

1 Mulch the garlic cloves around in a blender or food processor adding no water, or a minimum amount.
2 Scrape the garlic purée out of container, place in 10 ice-cube moulds and freeze raw.

GINGER PURÉE

In my previous book I stated that ginger has to be peeled before using. This is the way it has always been done. The skin of the ginger root causes a bitter taste, so it is said. But shortly after the first book was published I started to experiment and I have found that if ginger is mulched down it does not cause bitterness if the skin is left on. Remove the really rough ends or dirty bits, but leave any nice pink skin. It saves a great deal of time.

If you use dehydrated ginger, it must be soaked for several hours otherwise it is too hard.

**1 lb (450 g) fresh ginger,
   trimmed of hard knobs
   but unpeeled**

1 Coarsely chop the ginger then mulch it down in a blender or food processor.
2 Scrape out of container, place in 10 ice-cube moulds and freeze raw.

ONION PURÉE

Onions do not freeze whole at all well. As they are very watery, they become soggy when they thaw, which is fine for boiling and subsequent puréeing, but no use if you want to chop and fry them. Raw chopped and puréed onion freezes and thaws satisfactorily.

Unlike garlic and ginger, I find that onion needs to be boiled (blanched) in hot water first before puréeing, otherwise it has a very bitter taste.

**10 Spanish onions, about
   8 oz (225 g) each, peeled**

1 Coarsely chop the onions, and place them in boiling water. Strain after 3 minutes.
2 Mulch down in a blender or food processor until very fine in texture.
3 Scrape out of container, place in 10 yoghurt pots and freeze.

FRESH CORIANDER PURÉE

Fresh coriander is an essential ingredient for curry, contributing greatly to 'that restaurant taste'. The problems linked to it are twofold. Firstly, although it is flown in fresh from Cyprus, Egypt and Greece daily, and it is also grown in the UK, some greengrocers stubbornly refuse to stock it. If you have some of those in your town, go to your local curry house and ask which greengrocer supplies them. Whoever it is will supply coriander. Second, although it is not expensive, coriander comes in great big bunches. A lot can be wasted if it's not used within a day or so.

This purée is my solution, and it retains the original flavour almost as well as if it were fresh. As with all my purées I like to make up a large quantity then freeze it in ice-cube moulds, transferring the cubes to a rigid container later. Each cube gives enough coriander for an average recipe for four.

**4 bunches fresh coriander,
    washed and trimmed of
    coarse stalks**

$\frac{1}{2}$ **Spanish onion, peeled**

1 Chop the coriander coarsely, including the smaller stalks. Also chop the onion.

2 Put both into a food processor and mulch into a purée.

3 Scrape out and freeze in ice-cube trays.

An alternative to this purée method is simply to chop fresh coriander, dry it if necessary on kitchen paper, and freeze.

CURRY PASTES AND GRAVY

Anyone interested in Indian food must have encountered bottled curry pastes on the grocery shelves. There are many makes and types, but little explanation as to what they are or what they do. They are designed to take the labour out of blending a spice mixture, making it into a water paste and frying it. The manufacturers do it all for you, adding vinegar (acetic acid) and hot oil to prevent it from going mouldy. Unfortunately they also add salt and chilli powder which makes them a little overpowering. They are very concentrated, and you only need a small quantity for cooking.

Curry pastes are already cooked, but to 'disguise' them you will probably need to add some other whole or ground spices, and you will certainly need to fry garlic, ginger, onion, etc. Simply add the spice paste after these three are fried and carry on with the rest of the recipe.

HOME-MADE BOTTLED CURRY PASTE

The recipe below is for a mild paste which can form the base for many curry dishes. The quantities here will make a reasonable amount. Using vinegar (rather than all water) to make the paste will enable you to preserve it in jars. As with all pickling, sterilise the jars (a good hot wash in the dish washer followed by a dry out in a low-heat oven will do). Top off the paste in the jar with hot oil and inspect after a few days to see that there is no mould.

> **6–8 fl oz (175–250 ml) any vinegar**
> **6–8 fl oz (175–250 ml) vegetable oil**
> **250 g (1 recipe) mild curry powder (page 22)**

1 Mix together the curry powder spices.
2 Add the vinegar and enough water to make a creamy paste.
3 Heat the oil in a wok or karahi.
4 Add the paste to the oil. It will splutter a bit so be careful.
5 Stir fry the paste continually to prevent it sticking until the water content is cooked out (it should take about 5 minutes). As the liquid

is reduced, the paste begins to make a regular bubbling noise (hard to describe but it goes chup-chup-chup-chup) if you don't stir, and it will splatter. This is your audible cue that it is ready. You can tell if the spices are cooked by taking the karahi off the stove. Let stand for 3–4 minutes. If the oil 'floats' to the top, the spices are cooked. If not add a little more oil and repeat step 5.

6 Bottle the paste in sterilised jam jars.

7 Heat up a little more oil and 'cap' off the paste, by pouring in enough oil to cover the paste. Seal the jar and store.

GREEN MASALA PASTE

This is a kind of curry paste and it is green in colour because of its use of coriander and mint. You can buy it factory made, but it does not have the delicious fresh taste of this recipe from Ivan Watson, journalist and regular correspondent to The Curry Magazine. *You will come across green masala paste in the Indian home where it is used to enhance curry dishes and impart a subtle flavour that can be obtained in no other way.*

I have not specified its use in many of the following recipes, but you can add a heaped teaspoon in place of fresh coriander or garam masala towards the end of cooking virtually any dish. Try it on its own with potatoes: boil potatoes, add 1–1½ tablespoons of green masala paste, stir-fry and serve.

As with all curry pastes, this one will keep in jars indefinitely if made correctly.

1 teaspoon fenugreek seeds	3 teaspoons salt
6 cloves of garlic, chopped	3 teaspoons turmeric
2 tablespoons finely chopped fresh ginger	2 teaspoons chilli powder
	½ teaspoon ground cloves
1½ oz (40 g) fresh mint leaves	1 teaspoon ground cardamom
1½ oz (40 g) fresh coriander leaves	seeds
4 fl oz (100 ml) vinegar	4 fl oz (100 ml) vegetable oil
	2 fl oz (50 ml) sesame oil

1 Soak the fenugreek seeds in water overnight. They will swell and acquire a jelly-like coating.

2 Strain the fenugreek, discarding the water.

3 Mulch down all the ingredients, except the oils, in a blender or food processor, to make a purée.

4 To cook, follow the previous curry paste method.

CURRY MASALA GRAVY

Every curry restaurant has a large saucepan on the stove. In it is a pale orangey-gold gravy, quite thick in texture like apple purée. Taste and it's quite nice — a bit like a soup — or mild curry. Ask how it's made and like as not you'll get a shake of the head and a murmur about secrets of the trade. For this stock pot is one of the keys to achieving the restaurant curry. Recipes vary only slightly from chef to chef and restaurant to restaurant.

You can substitute this curry gravy for the individual garlic, ginger or onion purées given in many of the recipes which follow. Remember, this is just a mild base to which you can add other spices as required.

Here is the recipe used at two good curry restaurants — the **Balaka,** *133 Chanterlands Avenue, Hull, Humberside and the* **Viceroy of India,** *51 Sun Street, Biggleswade, Bedfordshire.*

$\frac{1}{2}$ **pint (300 ml) ghee or vegetable oil**

5 tablespoons garlic purée (page 25)

4 tablespoons ginger purée (page 26)

1 full recipe onion purée (page 26)

6 tablespoons tomato purée

1 teaspoon salt

Spices

2 tablespoons turmeric

4 tablespoons curry powder (page 22)

1–6 teaspoons chilli powder (to taste)

2 tablespoons ground cummin seeds

2 tablespoons finely chopped fresh coriander leaves

1 Mix the **Spices** with water to make a paste that has the approximate consistency of tomato ketchup. Let it stand whilst going to stage 2.

2 Heat the oil. Stir-fry the garlic purée for 3 minutes, then add the ginger purée and cook for 3 more minutes. Add the spice paste and stir-fry until the water has evaporated and the oil separates, about 5 minutes. Should it need it, add sufficient water to make the gravy pourable.

3 Add the onion purée and stir-fry for a further 10 minutes. Then add the tomato purée and stir-fry for a final 10 minutes. Add the salt.

4 Place into 10 moulds and freeze.

Makes *enough stock for 10 curries (40 portions)*

AKHNI STOCK

Some restaurants make a strained stock as well as or in place of the previous curry masala gravy. This flavoured clear liquid, sometimes called yakhni, is used exactly like any vegetable stock at any time the recipe directs 'add water'. You can keep it in the fridge for a couple of days, but it is essential to re-boil it after this time; it will be safe for several re-boils, but use it finally in a soup or other cooking. Add the brine or water from tinned vegetables to your stock. You can top it up with fresh or leftover ingredients as required.

This recipe is based on two in my collection, one from the **Indus Curry** *Tandoori Restaurant, 70A High Street, Colchester, Essex, the other from an Indian royal household. The ex-Maharaja of Sailana uses a similar liquid stock to which he adds raw meat off-cuts and bones for a non-vegetarian spicy stock.*

> 3 pints (1.7 litres) water
> 2 Spanish onions, peeled
>   and chopped
> 1 teaspoon garlic purée
> 1 teaspoon ginger purée
> 1 tablespoon ghee
> 2 teaspoons salt
>
> *Spices (whole)*
> 10 cloves
> 10 green cardamoms
> 6 pieces cassia bark
> 6 bay leaves

1 Boil the water then add everything else.

2 Simmer for 1 hour with the lid on, by which time the stock should have reduced by half.

3 Strain and discard the solids.

4 If you like, use 8 oz (225 g) meat off-cuts and bones at stage 2 in addition to the other ingredients.

CURRY BASES

Every restaurant is able, very quickly, to make up curry dishes at different heat strengths by using their curry masala gravy, spices and/or paste, and by adding their pre-cooked main ingredients. Hey presto, the 'instant' curry. The technique varies little from restaurant to restaurant, and it is useful for us to understand it and use it if we wish.

However, when we do have the time and inclination to produce individual curries with distinctive flavours, the best way is to cook them in more conventional ways as indicated in the recipes beginning at Chapter 3.

Meanwhile, here are the tricks of the trade from up and down the British Isles, which produce rich creamy curries of various heat strengths. Most curry restaurants in Britain are run by Bangladeshis, and they themselves do not enjoy hot curries. But really hot curries are popular and the restaurateurs are happy to meet the demand. Even if they could not eat them themselves, they have invented such fiery delights as the Madras curry, the vindaloo, bindaloo, tindaloo and the phal, sometimes enhanced by the name Bangalore phal. The Bangladeshi cook had probably never been near the southern Indian cities of Madras or Bangalore, or the Goan state where true vindaloo is practically the national dish. But with a relatively limited use of imagination, and an injudicious use of chilli powder and black pepper, the standard restaurant hot curries were born.

Once you have made your curry base add meat, chicken, vegetable or seafood to choice.

MILD CURRY BASE

This recipe is from the **Ganges,** *156 Fore Street, Exeter, Devon. They also have branches in Torbay, Truro and Plymouth.*

2 tablespoons ghee or vegetable oil

1 teaspoon garlic purée

1 tablespoon curry paste, *or* mild curry powder

$\frac{1}{2}$–$\frac{3}{4}$ pint (300–450 ml) curry masala gravy (page 30)

2 teaspoons tomato purée

1 teaspoon salt

akhni stock or water

1 Heat the ghee, and stir-fry the garlic for 1 minute.

2 Add the curry paste (or powder made into water paste), and stir-fry for 2 more minutes.

3 Add the masala gravy, using less if you want a dryish curry and more for a liquid sauce. Stir-fry for a couple of minutes then add the tomato purée and salt.

4 To obtain the wateriness you require, either add akhni stock or water to taste. (You may need to add a little oil as well to keep the correct texture.)

5 Add your principal ingredient – $1\frac{1}{2}$ lb (675 g) for 4 people – and when hot, serve.

Serves: 4

MEDIUM CURRY BASE

This recipe is also from a west country restaurant, the **Taj Mahal,** *63 Daniel Place, Lower Queen Street, Penzance, Cornwall. They also have a branch in Falmouth.*

1 recipe mild curry base (page 32)

$\frac{1}{2}$ **teaspoon turmeric**

$\frac{1}{2}$ **teaspoon chilli powder**

1 teaspoon aromatic garam masala

1 Proceed with stage 1 of the mild curry base (pages 32–3).

2 Add the spices. Stir-fry for 1 minute then add the curry paste and continue to the end of the method.

Serves: 4

MADRAS CURRY BASE

The Madras curry is the standard hot, slightly sour curry at the Indian restaurant. In reality there is no such dish as this in Madras (the largest city in southern India), and you won't find its recipe in any cookbook containing authentic recipes. But it is a very tasty dish if you enjoy a bit of a 'kick' with your food. Here is the recipe from the **Dilshad**, *41 Berry Street, Wolverhampton, West Midlands.*

1 recipe mild curry base (page 32)
$\frac{1}{2}$ teaspoon turmeric
$\frac{1}{2}$ teaspoon ground cummin
1 teaspoon ground black pepper
1 teaspoon chilli powder
$\frac{1}{2}$ Spanish onion, peeled and thinly sliced

4 fresh (or strained canned) tomatoes
2 teaspoons garam masala
1 tablespoon dry fenugreek leaves
1 tablespoon ground almonds
1 tablespoon fresh lemon juice, *or* bottied

1 Proceed with stage 1 of mild curry base (pages 32–3).
2 Make a water paste of the first four spices then add and fry in for 1 minute. Add the onion, and fry for 2 minutes.
3 Continue with stages 2 to 5 of mild curry base.
4 Add the fresh or canned tomatoes at the end of stage 5. When simmering add the remaining items.
5 Serve after a minimum of 5 minutes' simmering, or when ready.

Serves: 4

VINDALOO BASE

The true vindaloo comes from Goa, a tiny coastal state in south-western India. The restaurant vindaloo is very hot and contains a little vinegar (vin) and potato (aloo). This recipe is from the **Green Bengal** *restaurant, 68 The Green, Kings Norton, Birmingham. To make bindaloo or tindaloo add more chilli powder (or liquid chilli sauce).*

1 recipe mild curry base (page 32)
½ teaspoon turmeric
1 teaspoon ground black pepper
2–4 teaspoons chilli powder
½ Spanish onion, peeled and thinly sliced

6–8 × 2 inch (5 cm) pieces potato, boiled
2 teaspoons garam masala
1 tablespoon dry fenugreek leaves
1 tablespoon any vinegar

1 Proceed with stage 1 of mild curry base.
2 Make a water paste of the first three spices then add and fry in for 1 minute. Add the onion, stir-frying for 2 minutes.
3 Continue with stages 2 to 5 of mild curry base.
4 Add the potatoes and remaining ingredients at the end of stage 5.
5 Serve after a minimum of 5 minutes' simmering, or when ready.

Serves: 4

PHAL BASE

Pronounced pal *or* pol *and sometimes called Bangalore phal, this is the hottest curry the restaurants can make. There is nothing like it in India – it is pure invention. That's not to say they don't have hot curries in India, as the hottest curry I have ever had was in the southernmost part of India. It was a chilli curry and it used, I was told, six varieties of chilli including large mild green ones and tiny fierce red ones. The recipe apparently said 'take 30 chillies per person' . . .*

This recipe comes from the **Rupali** *restaurant, 6 Bigg Market, Newcastle, Tyne & Wear, and it is cooked so hot there that they issue a challenge that if you finish eating the entire dish you get it and a bottle of Indian beer free!!*

1 recipe mild curry base (page 32)
2 teaspoons ground black pepper
4 teaspoons chilli powder

1 tablespoon chopped chilli pickle from a bottle
any chilli sauce to taste (optional)

1 Proceed with stages 1 and 2 of mild curry base (pages 32–3).
2 Add the extra ingredients above and fry them in.
3 Carry on with stages 3 to 5.

Serves: 4

PRE-COOKED
MAIN CURRY INGREDIENT

In order to serve their enormous range and quantities, restaurants pre-cook their meat, chicken, potatoes, carrot and cauliflower. The requirement for the day is boiled in large saucepans in lightly spiced water until tender, then the ingredient is strained and cooled, and later used as required.

This technique can be applied in the home kitchen by using largish quantities and freezing the spare.

Here is the recipe from the **Surma,** *78 Broad Street, Ely, Cambridgeshire, for pre-cooked meat.*

**6 lb (2.7 kg) mutton or lamb,
cubed**

**3 tablespoons mild curry
powder (page 22)**

1 Place the meat and curry powder in a large lidded saucepan. Cover with water.

2 Bring to the boil and simmer for 40 minutes, stirring occasionally.

3 When tender (but not over-cooked), strain and cool and/or freeze in portions in freezer bags. (Although the restaurants discard the stock, I like to use it to make curry gravy.)

Enough for 4 curries of 4 servings each (16 portions)

TANDOORI COOKING

The tandoor oven is made of clay, cylindrical in shape and wider at the base than at the top. It has no bottom and a hole at the top. The clay is fashioned by hand and is strengthened by sacking. It is allowed to dry and is not 'fired'. It is merely put into place, often on or in the ground in the open air. Sizes vary: the biggest I've seen was about 4 feet (1.2 metres) high and the smallest $1\frac{1}{2}$ feet (45 cm). Quite where this type of oven was invented is lost to history: it may have been India, or it may have been the Middle East, where one encounters similar clay ovens called *tandir* or *tonir*. The tandoori boom in Britain took place during the 1970s when every restaurant claimed to be a tandoori house whether it owned a tandoor or not. But those days have gone and every restaurant usually has not one but two tandoors, one charcoal-fired running at temperatures of up to 700°F/371°C – the other gas-powered, operating at lower temperatures.

Despite wild claims from certain exuberant restaurant proprietors that they import their tandoors from India, most of them are made in England, in a purpose-built factory in London NW3. The factory makes small domestic tandoors exclusively for The Curry Club. We sell a good number of these each year, and this is part of a report from one user, Dr Richard Wood, who installed his tandoor permanently in his kitchen . . .

'The tandoori oven is a triumph of low technology. Everything about it is just right and works to perfection. The combustion of wood and charcoal occurs with an efficiency that I have never seen before, at high temperature with minimum heat loss. The actual cooking method is very fast baking (in fact on occasions the tandoor is almost as fast as a microwave). Food is skewered and the tip of the skewer sits in the charcoal. A good tip is to use an onion at the bottom as a stop. The heat derives from the oven environment, but also, and almost as important, much heat is conducted up the (quite thick) skewer to cook from the inside outwards. Chicken breasts or legs will cook in about 10–12 minutes. It is noticeable that bits of food near to the charcoal don't get any more browned (or charred) than bits at the top of the skewer near the mouth.'

The flavour of tandoori food is outstanding and unique, the result of a combination of the marinade and the very high temperature of the charcoal. Grilling on an ordinary barbecue will give almost the same flavours. Oven baking or grilling, however, is the way most of us at home will cook our tandooris and tikkas, and recipes in this book are written for these methods.

TANDOORI
DRY MIX MASALA

If you intend to make a lot of tandoori dishes it will be worth your while making up a batch of this spice masala. A dish for four requires a couple of tablespoons (around 30 g). This batch will fit in a large jar and be enough for about 40 individual portions (or 10 dishes for four). As with all pre-mixed masalas, it has the advantage of maturing during storage. Keep it in the dark in an airtight container, and it will be good for about 12 months.

45 g ($3\frac{1}{2}$ tablespoons) ground coriander

45 g ($3\frac{1}{2}$ tablespoons) ground cummin

45 g ($3\frac{1}{2}$ tablespoons) garlic powder

45 g ($3\frac{1}{2}$ tablespoons) paprika

25 g (5 teaspoons) ground ginger

25 g (5 teaspoons) mango powder

25 g (5 teaspoons) dried mint

25 g (5 teaspoons) beetroot powder (deep red colouring)*

20 g (4 teaspoons) chilli powder

10 g (1 teaspoon) anatto seed powder (yellow colouring)*

*If you use food colouring powder instead use only 5 g red (1 teaspoon) and 3 g sunset yellow ($\frac{1}{2}$ teaspoon). These small quantities will achieve a more vibrant colour than beetroot and annatto.

1 Simply mix the ingredients together well, and store.

2 To use, follow the tandoori/tikka recipes.

TANDOORI PASTE

Most restaurants use bright red tandoori paste to colour and spice their marinade. It is not difficult to make your own. To cook, use one recipe of the previous tandoori dry masala and cook it following the method for curry paste on pages 28–9.

TANDOORI OR TIKKA MARINADE

Yoghurt is used as the medium in which to 'suspend' the spices for tandoori or tikka marinade.

Here is the tikka marinade recipe from Nottingham's favourite, the **Mogal-e-Azam,** *7 Goldsmith Street, Royal Centre, Nottingham.*

Enough for 1½ lb (675 g) meat

5 oz (150 g) natural yoghurt

3 tablespoons mustard oil

2 tablespoons bottled or
   fresh lemon juice

1 teaspoon garlic purée

1 teaspoon ginger purée

3 fresh green chillies,
   chopped

1 tablespoon fresh mint or
   1 teaspoon bottled mint

3 tablespoons chopped
   fresh coriander leaves

1 teaspoon roasted cummin
   seeds, ground

1 teaspoon garam masala (page 42)

1 tablespoon curry paste (page 28)

2 tablespoons tandoori paste
   or dry mix masala (page 38)

1 teaspoon salt

Recipes using this marinade include Tandoori Sardines, Mutton and Chicken Tikka Masala, Tandoori Trout, Goan Duck and Aloo Makhanwala. (See index for page numbers.)

MISCELLANEOUS

The following recipes don't strictly come into any of the previous categories, so are headed as above – they're anything but 'miscellaneous' in curry cooking though!

GHEE

Ghee is a clarified butter, which is very easy to make and gives a distinctive and delicious taste. When cooled and set, it will keep for several months without refrigeration.

If you want to make vegetable ghee, simply use block margarine instead of butter.

2 lb (900 g) any butter

1   Place the butter blocks whole into a medium non-stick pan. Melt at a very low heat.

2   When completely melted, raise heat very slightly. Ensure it does not smoke or burn, but don't stir. Leave to cook for about 1 hour. The impurities will sink to the bottom and float on the top. Carefully skim off the floating sediment with a slotted spoon, but don't touch the bottom.

3   Turn off the heat and allow the ghee to cool a little. Then sieve it through kitchen paper or muslin into an airtight storage jar. When it cools it solidifies, although it is quite soft. It should be a bright pale lemon colour and it smells like toffee. If it has burned it will be darker and smell different. Providing it is not too burned it can still be used.

PANEER CHEESE

This is a fresh home-made cheese which does not melt when cooked. It is full of protein and easy to make. It resembles compacted cottage cheese and is very common in the sub-continent as a vegetarian dish.

Makes about 8 oz (225 g)

4 pints (2.25 litres) full-
    cream milk (not UHT)

4–6 tablespoons any
    vinegar, *or* lemon juice

1 Choose a large pan. If you have one of 12 pint (6.75 litres) capacity, the milk will only occupy a third of the pan and won't boil over (unless the lid is on).

2 Bring the milk slowly to the boil. Add the vinegar or lemon juice, stirring until it curdles – when the curds separate from the whey.

3 Strain into a clean teatowel placed on a strainer over a saucepan. Fold the teatowel over and press the excess liquid – the whey – through. Keep for later use as stock.

4 Now place the curds – from now on called paneer – on to the draining board still in the teatowel. Press it out to a circle about $\frac{1}{2}$ inch (1.25 cm) thick. Place a flat weight (the original saucepan full of water for instance) on the teatowel, and allow it to compress the paneer.

5 If you want crumbly paneer (as for page 133), remove the weight after 30–45 minutes. Crumble the paneer and use as the recipe directs.

6 If you want the paneer to be solid, keep the weight on for $1\frac{1}{2}$–2 hours. Then cut the paneer into cubes.

7 Cubed paneer is normally deep-fried to a pale golden colour for best texture.

TAMARIND PURÉE

Tamarind — also known as the Indian date — is a major souring agent, particularly in southern Indian cooking. The tamarind tree bears pods of about 6–8 inches (15–20 cm) long which become dark brown when ripe. These pods contain seeds and pulp, which are preserved indefinitely for use in cooking by compression into a rectangular block weighing about 11 oz (300 g).

To use the tamarind block, soak it overnight in twice its volume of hot water — about 23 fl oz (650 ml) per 11 oz (300 g) block. The next day pulp it well with your fingers, then strain through a sieve, discarding the husks. The brown liquid should be quite thick, and there will be plenty of it. Freeze any spare.

GARAM MASALA

Garam means hot and masala means mixture of spices, and there are as many combinations and recipes of garam masala as there are cooks who make it. Some use only five or six spices and I have one recipe which lists as many as fifteen spices! This one has only nine and has been my favourite for years. Try it. For the next batch, you might like to vary the mixture to your own preference. That's the fun of Indian cookery. (Again I list in metric only, as that's the only way I weigh out the spices for this, and it doesn't transfer easily into Imperial.)

This particular garam masala is available from The Curry Club.

For an aromatic *garam masala, use this recipe without* the pepper corns *and* ginger.

(I came across a remarkably 'mild' garam masala recipe in Kashmir which uses no hot spices at all. In their place were saffron stamens and rose petals. If you wish to use saffron add it whole at the very end of cooking.)

110 g coriander seeds	**30 g brown cardamoms**
110 g cummin seeds	**15 g nutmeg**
50 g black peppercorns	**10 g bay leaves**
30 g cassia bark	**15 g ground ginger**
30 g cloves	

1 Lightly roast everything except the ground ginger under a low to medium heat grill, or in an oven at about 325°F/160°C/Gas 3. Do not let the spices burn. They should give off a light steam.

2 When they give off an aroma — in the oven, 10 minutes is enough — remove from the heat, cool and grind. A coffee grinder will do if you use small quantities, and break up large items first.

3 After grinding add the ground ginger, mix thoroughly and store in an airtight jar. Garam masala will last almost indefinitely, but it is always better to make small fresh batches every few months to get the best flavours.

CHAR MASALA

Char in Hindi, Urdu and Afghan means four, and masala, our familiar mixture of spices. This is to Afghan cooking what garam masala is to Indian. Use it in the Afghan recipes in this book, or as a substitute for garam masala if you wish to have a very fragrant mixture of spices with no heat.

The four spices are usually the same, though the proportions can vary. This very fragrant recipe makes 60 g worth (enough for four curries)

    20 g cassia bark
    20 g white cummin seeds
    10 g green cardamom seeds
       (not pods)
    10 g cloves

Roast, grind and store in a jam jar.

PANCH PHORAN

This is a Bengali mixture of five (panch) spices. There are several possible combinations. This is my favourite. Use it in vegetable cooking, for example Niramish on page 132.

Mix together equal parts of (a teaspoon of each is plenty):

    white cummin seeds   mustard seeds
    fennel seeds   wild onion seeds
    fenugreek seeds

3
STARTERS

A meal of several courses is a Western concept born
in an age gone by and brought to its height in Vic-
torian times when course would follow course, and
tables and diners would groan from the sheer weight
of so much food.

In many parts of traditional India the convention
of courses is unknown. The complete meal is served
at once – soups (thin curries), masalas (thick curries),
rissoles and pastries, breads, rice and lentils and
sweets appear together each in a strictly pre-
determined place. Most of the people of village India
adhere to this tradition. The minority city-dwelling
middle class (some 80 million, none-the-less) have
adopted Western conventions and are content to eat
in two or three courses. Bengalis enjoy several
courses, but it is the Parsee community who cap
everything with up to 20 courses at their formal
dinners.

KUDI II
Gujerati Soup

The first contact the English made with India was in 1608 when a Captain
Hawkins, a sailor in the employ of King James I, landed in the north-western
state of Gujerat. Whether Hawkins tried the food of this mainly vegetarian
state is not on record, but if he had he would certainly have tasted kudhi. It
is a soup traditionally but optionally containing whey and gram flour dumplings in its tasty sour and spicy yoghurt base.

Kudhi, also called kari, is one of the possible derivatives of the word 'curry'
given to the world by the English. This recipe is from the health-conscious
Gujerati **Deansgate** Indian Restaurant, 224 Deansgate, Manchester.

2 tablespoons ghee or
    vegetable oil

10 oz (275 g) natural
    yoghurt

2 tablespoons gram flour
    (besan)

1 teaspoon ginger purée

1–4 green chillies, chopped

$\frac{1}{2}$ teaspoon salt

1 pint (600 ml) water or
    akhni stock (or paneer
    whey, page 41)

2 teaspoons brown sugar

Spices

1 teaspoon mustard seeds

$\frac{1}{2}$ teaspoon fenugreek seeds

6 dry curry leaves

a pinch of asafoetida

1 Heat the ghee or oil and fry all the **Spices** for 2 minutes in a
   saucepan large enough for the whole job.

2 Mix the yoghurt and gram flour, then add the remaining ingredients.
   Stir in well. Place everything into the saucepan.

3 Simmer for 20 minutes, stirring from time to time.

4 Serve hot as a soup on its own or as a thin curry gravy with rice.

Serves: 4

MOHINGA
Spicy Noodle Fish Soup

Burmese food is quite distinctive and unique, and sadly little known. It has evolved into a combination of Indian (robust and hot spicing), Chinese (noodles, beansprouts, stir-frying) and Thai (fragrance and fish sauces). If one recipe is to be singled out to typify Burma it must be mo-hi-nga — literally noodle-spicy-fish soup. Indeed, it is referred to as the national dish. In Burma you buy mohinga from roadside stalls or from vendors who back-pack their cooking apparatus and ingredients from house to house. It is a spicy, tart, fishy soup with a fascinating string of garnishes. The Burmese eat it as a complete main meal, but it also makes an ideal starter. The ingredients list looks a little formidable, but it is much simpler to make than it looks. This superb recipe comes from Britain's one and only Burmese restaurant, the **Mandalay***, 100 Greenwich South Street, London SE10.*

2 tablespoons mustard or
   sesame oil

2 teaspoons garlic purée

8 tablespoons onion purée

1 teaspoon *nga-pi* (shrimp
   paste)

1–6 (to taste) fresh green
   chillies, chopped

3 tablespoons gram flour
   (besan)

3 tablespoons coconut
   powder

1 × 7 oz (200 g) can
   pilchards or herrings,
   boned

1 × 8 oz (225 g) can bamboo
   shoots

akhni stock or water

juice of 2 lemons

salt to taste

100 g (4 oz) egg or
   vermicelli noodles

Garnishes
hard-boiled egg slices
chopped spring onion leaf
chopped fresh coriander
   leaves
watercress or mustard and
   cress
tiny prawn pakoras (lentil
   flour fritters)
julienne of capsicum
   peppers (red, green or
   yellow)

1 Heat the oil, and fry the garlic for 1 minute, then add the onion and fry for 3 minutes. Add the *nga-pi* and mash and fry for 2 minutes, followed by the chillies for 2 minutes.

2 Mix the gram flour and coconut powder with enough water to make a thick paste. Add to the pan and stir over heat until it will thicken no more.

3 Transfer to a saucepan. Break the fish up, and add it and juices. Add chopped bamboo shoots and can juices.

4 Add enough vegetable stock or water to bring it to consommé consistency, then add the lemon juice and salt to taste.

5 Cook the noodles in a separate pan. Follow the packet instructions which normally simply require them to be immersed in boiling water, then left to one side for about 8 minutes until tender. Drain.

6 To serve, place the noodles in a soup bowl and ladle the piping hot soup over them. Serve, allowing the diners to put their own choice of garnish items on to the soup.

Serves: 4

ASHAK
Pastry Filled with Leek,
Spicy Mince and Yoghurt

Afghanistan has had the misfortune of being a through-way between Persia and the sub-continent. In fact, apart from sea routes, the passes through Afghanistan were the only way to reach India. Not surprisingly Afghan food includes Iranian and Indian influences with such dishes as biriani and curries, but it also has a distinctive style of its own. Ashak is a lovely Afghan speciality and it will be found at either of London's two Afghan restaurants, the **Afghan Buzkash***, 4 Chelverton Road, London SW15 or its sister,* **The Caravan Serai***, 50 Paddington Street, London W1. It consists of crescent-shaped stuffed pastries, boiled dumpling style, and served in a spicy gravy. The filling traditionally consists of Chinese chives or* gandana*, a type of long grass not unlike our leeks. Gandana is very occasionally available here but you can substitute leeks, ordinary chives and/or spring onions.*

Dough
1 lb (450 g) plain white flour
1 tablespoon vegetable oil
1 egg

Filling
12 oz (350 g) leek leaves, or
  spring onions, chives or
  a combination
1 garlic clove
2 tablespoons chopped
  fresh coriander leaves
$\frac{1}{2}$ teaspoon salt
$\frac{1}{2}$ teaspoon ground black
  pepper

Gravy
3 tablespoons vegetable oil
1 teaspoon garlic purée
4 tablespoons onion purée
6 oz (175 g) lamb or beef,
  minced *or* soya mince for
  vegetarians
1 tablespoon char masala
6 fresh tomatoes
1 tablespoon tomato purée
salt to taste

Garnish
natural yoghurt or soured
  cream
chopped fresh coriander

1 To make up the dough, mix the flour with the oil, egg and a little water – enough to create a smooth pliable dough. Let it rest for at least 1 hour.

2 Meanwhile, make the filling. Mulch up the leaves, coriander, salt and pepper either in a mortar or in a food processor. Do not make it into a purée – rather just pulse it a few times, then put it into a strainer to drain.

3 Start making the gravy about half an hour before you want to serve the ashaks. Heat the oil, and fry the garlic for 1 minute, then add the onion and fry for 3 minutes. Add the mince and the char masala spices. Stir-fry for a further 10 minutes, then add the tomatoes and tomato purée. Simmer until ready to serve – for a minimum of 10 minutes – then add salt to taste.

4 Knead the dough well, and roll out very thin, to about 1/16 inch (1.5 mm) for light ashaks (the thicker the pastry the chewier the ashaks will be). Cut into 4 inch (10 cm) circles using a saucer or cutter. Re-roll spare pastry as necessary, trying to get 8 circles. (I got 10 the last time, with very thin pastry.)

5 Place 1 tablespoon of the filling on half of the circle then fold it over, tweaking the edges to seal it well. Shape it to the traditional crescent shape. Do the same with the remainder of the circles.

6 Place them at once into a pan of simmering water. Carefully remove after 10 minutes.

7 Place at once on to a serving bowl. Top with the hot gravy, then garnish with the yoghurt or soured cream and fresh coriander.

Makes *8 small dumplings*

ALOO-ACHAR
Cold potato pickle

Aloo or alu means potato and achar is pickle. This cold dish, spiced with pickle and yoghurt, is sour and tangy in taste. It hails from the Himalayan mountain country of Nepal, from whence come those hardy sherpahs (who enable Everest expeditions to succeed) and ghurkas (the fierce fighting troops so highly prized in the British army). Two other tough individuals live here — the mysterious yeti and the shaggy yak, beast of burden and milk and meat supply. In the bitterly cold winters the Nepalese rely on their supply of dried foods and pickles. This dish is typical and the recipe is from the particularly good **Johnnie Gurkha's Restaurant**, *186 Victoria Road, Aldershot, Hampshire. The very name tells you that it is Nepalese, and its address that it caters to the British army, with Gurkha HQ a mere 'chupatti' throw away.*

1 lb (450 g) potatoes, boiled
2 tablespoons mustard oil
1 teaspoon black mustard seed
2 teaspoons white sesame seed
1 teaspoon white poppy seed
1 teaspoon garlic purée
2 tablespoons onion purée
2 tablespoons fresh coriander
2 teaspoons dried mint
2 tablespoons curry paste
2 tablespoons brinjal pickle, chopped up
salt to taste

1 Cool and dice the potato into $\frac{1}{2}$ inch (1.25 cm) cubes.

2 Heat the oil. Stir-fry the seeds (1 minute), the garlic purée (a further minute) and the onion purée (2 more minutes).

3 Add a drop of water to ease any sticking, then put in the remaining ingredients, including the diced potato. Stir round well and remove from the heat. It should be dry. Serve cold.

***Serves:* 4**

ALOO TAMA
Potato Cooked with Bamboo Shoots

This is another Nepalese dish and comes from chef Gopal Dangol of the **Kathmandu** *restaurant, 442 Sackville Street, Manchester M1.*

12 oz (350 g) new potatoes
2 tablespoons vegetable oil
1 teaspoon garlic purée
1 teaspoon ginger purée
4 tablespoons onion purée
4 oz (100 g) bamboo shoots, canned or fresh
1–4 fresh chillies, chopped (to taste)
2 tablespoons chopped fresh coriander leaves
2 fl oz (50 ml) single cream
salt to taste

Spices
3 cloves
1 inch (2.5 cm) piece cassia bark
1 teaspoon white cummin seeds
1 teaspoon paprika

1 Scrub the potatoes and boil until nearly done. Drain and leave to cool.

2 Whilst they are boiling, heat the oil and fry the **Spices** for 1 minute, the puréed garlic for 1 minute, the ginger purée for 2 minutes, and the onion purée for 3 minutes.

3 Dice the potatoes and bamboo shoots and add them to the pan with enough water, *and no more*, to allow them to simmer. Add the chilli, coriander and cream. Simmer for enough time to finish the cooking of the potato. Add salt to taste.

Serves: *4*

CHANA CHAT
Chickpea curry

Chat pronounced 'chart' and sometimes spelt 'chaat' means snack or appetiser in Hindi, and this chickpea dish is particularly good cold with crispy papadoms or deep-fried puri bread. It is nice hot, too, as this recipe from **Light of India, 33 Woodford Avenue, Gant's Hill, Ilford** *shows.*

8 oz (225 g) chickpeas

2 tablespoons vegetable oil

1 teaspoon white cummin seeds

2 teaspoons white sesame seeds

1 teaspoon white poppy seeds

1 teaspoon garlic purée

2 tablespoons onion purée

2 tablespoons fresh coriander

1 teaspoon dried mint

1 teaspoon dried fenugreek leaves

1 tablespoon curry paste

1 tablespoon tandoori paste

2 fresh tomatoes, chopped

1 tablespoon tomato purée

5 fl oz (140 ml) tomato soup (canned)

salt to taste

1 Check that the chickpeas are free of grit, then rinse them and soak them in twice their volume of water for 6–24 hours.

2 Strain the chickpeas, rinse with cold water, then boil them in ample water for 40–45 minutes until tender.

3 About 5 minutes before they are ready, heat the vegetable oil. Stir fry the seeds (1 minute), then add the garlic purée and cook for a further minute, and then add the onion purée and fry for 2 more minutes. Add all the remaining ingredients. Stir fry for about 5 minutes.

4 Strain the chickpeas and add them to the sauce. Remove from heat and serve hot or allow to cool.

Serves: *4 as a starter*

SHEEK KEBAB
Minced Beef Cooked on Skewers

Kebabs are said to have originated in Turkey, indeed the word means 'cooked meat' in Turkish. Shish means 'skewer' and this has become sis, sheesh or sheek as the method migrated eastwards into India. Mutton would have been the traditional meat, pounded on the grinding stone with the roots and spices. Many tandoori restaurants use beef. Use either a food processor or mincer to achieve a mouldable, glutinous texture.

This recipe is to be found with minor variations all over the sub-continent and in curry restaurants all over the world. Here is the method from the **Rajpoot** *restaurant, 4 Argyle Street, Bath, Avon. The kebab mixture is also used for the filling of keema naan (page 161).*

$1\frac{1}{2}$ lb (675 g) top side, or
fillet steak (the better the
meat the better the kebab)

4–6 garlic cloves, chopped

1 inch (2.5 cm) piece fresh
ginger, chopped

2–4 fresh green chillies,
chopped (to taste)

2 tablespoons chopped
fresh coriander leaves

1 teaspoon garlic powder

1 teaspoon dried mint

1 tablespoon curry paste

1 teaspoon tandoori paste

1 Inspect the meat. Remove fat, skin and gristle if any. Chop it coarsely.

2 Mix the meat well with all the other ingredients, then process or mince it to a fine texture.

3 Mix it all again, using the fingers – it's messy, but the fingers are a chef's best tools! Divide into four (or eight).

4 Using metal skewers, shape each portion of mince on the skewer into a long sausage of about 6 inches (15 cm). The smaller kebabs should be about 3 in (7.5 cm) in length.

5 Preheat the oven to 190°C/375°F/Gas 5, place the kebabs on an oven tray and bake for 15 minutes. Or use a grill at about three-quarters heat, rotating the kebabs a few times.

6 Serve on a bed of lettuce with a lemon wedge and chutneys.

Makes *4 large or 8 smaller kebabs*

RASHMI KEBAB
Kebab in an Egg Net

This is a finely minced or ground lamb or beef kebab wrapped inside a net-like omelette casing. The net casing itself requires a little practice and patience, and an altogether much simpler method is to make a very thin omelette and wrap the kebab inside. The net appears in many oriental dishes from Afghanistan to Thailand. It is interesting to attempt and once mastered you have a dish which looks professional and unusual.

This recipe is from **The Star of Asia***, 237 Cowley Road, Oxford. Their kebab method is very similar to other restaurants, so use the previous sheek kebab recipe.*

1 recipe sheek kebab
   (previous recipe)
vegetable oil for deep-
   frying

Net
2 large eggs, beaten

1 Divide the kebab mixture into four.

2 Shape into small flat circles (flying saucers) and cook as for sheek kebabs in the previous recipe.

3 To make the egg net, heat plenty of oil in a deep-frying pan to 160°F/325°C. Test with a 'flick' of egg which should float sizzling, but not burn. Then drip the egg off the fingers, slowly moving across the pan to form a grid. Use about $\frac{1}{2}$ an egg per grid. Lift the grid out as soon as it is formed and wrap it around the cooked kebab. Repeat three more times.

Makes *4 kebabs*

NARGISSI KOFTA KE BAHAR
Indian 'Scotch Egg'

Scotch egg is the best way to visualise this dish. The traditional meat is ground mutton, but as with the previous kebab recipe, beef is acceptable wrapped around a hard-boiled chicken egg, and this is the way they do it at **The British Raj**, *55 High Street, Royston, Hertfordshire.*

I have developed a very interesting variation for this dish. Instead of red meat, I use chicken breast wrapped around a hard-boiled chicken or duck egg. My favourite variation uses quail eggs (note the short boiling time) for really dainty koftas – serve two per person.

8 quail (or 4 chicken or duck) eggs

8–12 oz (225–350 g) chicken breast, skinned and boned

1 inch (2.5 cm) cube fresh ginger

2 garlic cloves

2–4 fresh chillies (optional, to taste)

1 tablespoon chopped fresh coriander leaves

4 tablespoons semolina

vegetable oil

Spices (ground)

$\frac{1}{2}$ teaspoon cummin

$\frac{1}{2}$ teaspoon coriander

$\frac{1}{2}$ teaspoon paprika

$\frac{1}{2}$ teaspoon garam masala

2 teaspoons dry fenugreek leaves

1 teaspoon curry paste

1 Hard-boil the quail eggs for about 4 minutes in boiling water (15 minutes for chicken or duck eggs) then run under cold water. To prevent them cracking, ensure they are at room temperature and prick the blunt end with a pin before boiling.

2 Chop the chicken breast and the ginger, garlic and chilli (optional but nice) and place all this with the **Spices** and fresh coriander into a food processor. Make this mixture into a coarse purée by pulsing.

3 Divide the mixture into eight (or four) and wrap it around the shelled eggs, achieving a round or egg shape. Roll the shapes in the semolina and place on an oven tray. Glaze with oil.

4 Preheat the oven to 375°F/190°C/Gas 5. When hot put the tray in and bake for 15 minutes. Serve hot.

Serves: *4*

SHASHLIK KEBAB

Shashlik *literally means 'meat and vegetables on a skewer'. The word comes from the Russian (Armenian) 'to grill'. The shashlik method no doubt travelled from the Middle East, through Iran (where the same style of cooking is called the hasina kebab) and eventually into India. As far as the method goes, it is straightforward, and has probably been around as long as cooking itself. What could be easier than to pick up a piece of meat on the tip of a sword and grill it over fire? Here I use bamboo skewers.*

This version is from one of the best restaurants in Wales, the **Everest***, 43 Salisbury Road, Cardiff. Served on a bed of lettuce, topped with mustard and cress, parsley, coriander and a lemon or lime wedge, it not only looks great but is healthy, being low in calories and high in proteins and vitamins, especially if you eat the garnish salad.*

either **16 × 1 inch (2.5 cm) cubes skinned chicken breast,** *or* **16 similarly sized pieces lamb (or a combination)**
$\frac{1}{2}$ **each of red pepper, green pepper and yellow pepper, seeded**
1 Spanish onion, peeled

4 lemon or lime wedges
4 green chillies (optional)

Marinade
6 tablespoons mustard oil
1 teaspoon garlic powder
1 tablespoon dried mint
1 tablespoon curry paste
$\frac{1}{2}$ **tablespoon salt**

1 Immerse the diced chicken or lamb in the marinade for 24 hours.

2 Strain off the surplus marinade. If barbecuing, place the meat or chicken on metal skewers and heat over charcoal for 10–15 minutes for chicken, 20–25 minutes for lamb. If grilling, place the meat or chicken on foil on the grill pan located on middle slot under moderate grill. Cook for the same times, turning once or twice. With either method, baste occasionally with marinade.

3 During the cooking, cut the three peppers into 1 inch (2.5 cm) diamond shapes, and the onion the same.

4 Once the meat or chicken is cooked, transfer it to 4 bamboo skewers (if hot, use tongs), interspersed with the peppers, onion, lemon wedge and a chilli. Finish off over charcoal or under grill until sizzling and fully hot. Serve at once on a bed of lettuce and onion rings.

Serves: 4

BENGALI FISH KEBABS

Bengal is a Hindu state in the north-east of India. It shares its border, and India's most sacred river, the Ganges, with Bangladesh (formerly East Bengal), now an independent Muslim state. It was religion which divided Bengal in 1947, but the culinary tradition of both Bengals remains identical, and the fish from the Ganges and Hougli rivers and the Bay of Bengal are prolific and important. Unfortunately, although a great many of Britain's curry restaurateurs are Bangladeshi, they rarely depart from the standard well-proven curry formula to bring their diners authentic dishes from the Bengal area. One owner/chef who does is Tommy Miah, who has the distinction at the age of 28 of owning two Edinburgh restaurants and of having written his own cookbook. Here is one of Tommy's superb recipes as served in **The Raj**, *Henderson Street, Leith, near Edinburgh, Lothian.*

1 lb (450 g) cod steaks
1 teaspoon garlic purée
1 teaspoon ginger purée
2 tablespoons onion purée
1–4 chillies, chopped (to
    taste)
5 oz (150 g) natural yoghurt
salt to taste
1 teaspoon turmeric
2 teaspoons garam masala
ghee for basting

1 Cut the fish into 1 inch (2.5 cm) cubes. Wash, drain and dry them.
2 Mix all the remaining ingredients, except for the ghee, to form a marinade paste. Marinade the cubes in this for 2 hours or so.
3 Thread the fish on to 4 bamboo skewers, and grill as in the previous shashlik recipe for 10 minutes. Then baste with ghee and serve on a bed of salad.

Serves: 4

MAACHLI QUTABSHAI
Dry Spicy Fried Fish

Satish Arora is Director of Cuisine of one of the world's most prestigious hotel and restaurant groups – Taj Hotels Ltd. Based at their flagship, the incomparable **Taj Mahal Intercontinental Hotel** *in Bombay, Chef Arora is responsible for 1,500 chefs worldwide (the group owns Britain's number one Indian restaurant, The Bombay Brasserie) at their 30 or so hotels. He is also responsible for supplying a number of airlines with in-flight catering at Bombay's international airport. At the Taj Hotel, his executive chef has under him a kitchen brigade of 150, working 24 hours a day supplying the eleven restaurants and banqueting suites. Whether it is Indian, Chinese, French, nouveau, fast food or room service, it comes under the control of chef Arora. It is nothing for the hotel to prepare 5,000 meals in a day. Two roles he greatly enjoys are chef training – at any one time he has 40 apprentices under him – and developing a new style of Indian cuisine, using a combination of traditional Indian spicing techniques and ideas from Europe. Not only are his creations delightful but the concept is brilliant.*

This dish, its name from maachi *(fish) and* qutabshai *(dedicated to a twelfth-century Afghan-Turkish conqueror who raised the status of Delhi from provincial town to fortress capital), gives a whole new insight into fish cooked in batter. But you can, of course, use shellfish, chicken, other white meat or vegetables.*

8 fish fillets (use sole or
   plaice)
4 tablespoons vinegar
juice of 2 lemons
salt to taste
vegetable oil, for deep-
   frying

Batter
5 oz (150 g) gram flour
   (besan)
5 oz (150 g) plain white
   flour
1 teaspoon garlic purée
1 teaspoon white cummin
   seeds
1 teaspoon carraway seeds
4 tablespoons chopped
   fresh coriander leaves
0–4 green chillies, chopped
   (to taste)
3 eggs
salt to taste

1 Wash the fish fillets and marinate in the vinegar, lemon juice and salt for 30 minutes.

2 Strain the fish, reserving the marinade. Make the batter by simply mixing all the batter ingredients together with the reserved marinade. By using no water, it will be crisper.

3 Dip the fish in the batter and half fry, until it starts to crisp. Remove from the oil, set aside for a few minutes, then fry again until golden brown.

Serves: 4

PRAWN PATHIA AND PURI

Pathia is a dry-fried sweet and sour dish from Bombay's Parsee community. It goes beautifully with prawns. Puri are the small brown flour bread discs which, when deep-fried, puff up like little balloons. The prawn pathia is simply stir-fried and placed on the puri, garnished with fresh coriander, and served piping hot. This recipe comes from Britain's southernmost restaurant, **The Light of India,** *6 Cheapside, Jersey, Channel Islands.*

1 lb (450 g) shelled, deveined prawns (you want them as small as possible, so ask for 200–300 per 1 lb/450 g)

4 tablespoons ghee or vegetable oil

2 teaspoons garlic purée

6 tablespoons onion purée

2 tablespoons curry paste

1 tablespoon coconut powder

1 tablespoon tomato purée

2 teaspoons prawn ballachung (prawn pickle)

$1\frac{1}{2}$ tablespoons jaggery or brown sugar

salt to taste

chopped fresh coriander leaves

1 Prepare and wash the prawns. Drain and set aside.
2 Heat the ghee or oil, and fry the purées for 5 minutes, then add the remaining ingredients including the prawns.
3 Simmer for 10 minutes, adding enough water to prevent sticking.
4 Make the puris as on page 163.
5 Serve on the puris, and garnish with some coriander.

Serves: 4

PRAWN BUTTERFLIES

Two things make this dish remarkable in a restaurant. First, they use gigantic fresh water 'shrimps' from the river Ganges imported frozen (and now becoming widely available). At around 4 oz (100 g) each in weight and measuring some 5 inches (13 cm), they are substantial in size, and firm in texture. Second, by 'fanning' the tail before dipping in the batter, the butterfly appearance is achieved. Here is the method from the **Bengal Lancer**, *253 Kentish Town Road, London NW5. This excellent restaurant is named in memory of the days when Britain ruled the seas and its Indian Empire. The latter it did effectively with its highly mobile front-line troops – the cavalry. The first unit was formed in 1774 to protect the Governor-General of Bengal. At the height of the Raj there were 40 cavalry regiments. One still remains today, incorporated into the modern Indian army for ceremonial duties.*

> **4 large prawns, around 4 oz**
>   **(100 g) each**
> **batter (page 58)**

1 Carefully de-head, shell and de-vein the prawns, but keep the tail shells on them. Fan out the tails and flatten them with a cleaver.

2 Immerse the prawns entirely into the batter and deep fry at 375°F/190°C for about 10 minutes.

3 Serve at once on a bed of salad, otherwise the batter goes soggy and chewy.

Serves: 4

TANDOORI SARDINES

I needed an attractive starter for a Curry Club function and it occurred to me that sardines have been completely overlooked at the Indian restaurant. I can't imagine why because, baked tandoori-style, they are perfect.

8 sardines 2 oz (50 g) each
tandoori marinade

1 Keep the fish whole. Wash and dry them.
2 Leave the sardines in the marinade for 2 hours.
3 Oven-bake them in a pan in an oven pre-heated to 325°F/160°C/Gas 3 for about 30 minutes. This length of time should caramelise the marinade without overcooking the fish. You could grill the fish on medium heat or, of course, barbecue them. Serve on a bed of salad.

Serves: *4*

4
MEAT

Contrary to popular belief, meat eating is quite widespread in India, especially amongst certain groups.
Most of the Indian population is Hindu, to whom the
cow is sacred. Those who do eat meat, enjoy mutton
and goat; they would have no aversion to eating pork,
but rarely get the opportunity to do so. Hindus would
not eat beef or veal.

The worship of the cow pre-dates the establishment
of the Hindu religion. In fact it goes back to the
nomadic cattle-breeding tribes of Aryans who entered
India around 1500 BC displacing the literate and very
civilised Harrapan incumbents of the Indus valley.
The Aryans originated in the Caucasus, and branches
spread west as far as the Danube and east as far as
China, and across the Levant to Iran (to whom they
bequeathed the country's name) and on through into
north India. With them went their herds of cattle.
These they farmed and used not only for dairy products, but for leather and for meat. As the tribes grew
and diversified, their descendants gradually changed
the emphasis more to dairy farming and less to meat.
This may well have been because of shortages of
livestock. Eventually the Hindu religion emerged; the
cow became venerated and was no longer eaten.

The Islamic laws relating to food are very similar
to those of Judaism. Jews must only eat food which

is kosher (fit and proper), whilst to Moslems it must be halal (clean). To fail to eat thus would be unthinkable to true practitioners of both religions. Kosher and halal food must be prepared and eaten according to unbreakable rules. Meat must be slaughtered then cut in a particular way, and blood must not be present in the meat ready for cooking.

Common to both religions is a proscription on the eating of pork. The animal is considered to be unclean, its flesh the carrier of disease, and a strict orthodox Jew or Moslem would be unable to contemplate its consumption. The origins of this are obscure. Uncleanliness and disease are not satisfactory reasons – pork has been the primary meat of the Far East for millenia – and the true answer may lie in the fact that pigs, being rooters, simply did not thrive in desert conditions. The few that did, apart from being scarce, may well have been diseased. Jews are not permitted to eat rabbit, shellfish or any meat cooked or served with dairy products, but these rules do not apply to Moslems. The Iranians, on the other hand, developed a style of cooking in which meat is marinated in yoghurt, undoubtedly originating from the time of the Aryans. It is a technique widely used in the northern curry lands to this day.

The most popular meats eaten by Moslems are mutton or goat (lamb being a luxury for special occasions), and chicken. Beef is permitted and enjoyed, although cattle in the form of cows, oxen or buffalo are uncommon. Horse meat is as unlikely to be eaten on the sub-continent as it is in the UK although the Mongols from whom the Moghul emperors were descended undoubtedly ate horse. The Moghuls almost certainly did not.

The pig could thrive in many parts of India but few are to be seen except in Goa. Goans are Christian Indians and they adore pork. Pork has always been the number one meat in Burma, Thailand, Indo-China and China. The Chinese, by the way, eat beef as well, but rarely mutton. They detest all dairy products especially milk which they regard as an offensive-smelling liquid about as appetising as saliva. But then they eat dog and locusts ... it's a strange world.

SULTANI PASANDA
Beaten Sliced Meat Curry

Pasanda means 'beaten'. Traditionally mutton would be used, but beef gives much better results, as we are able to get such excellent quality beef. Veal, lamb, even duck breast, can be used with equal success in this superb recipe from the elegant **Sultani Restaurant,** *Horse Street, Chipping Sodbury.*

$1\frac{1}{2}$ lb (675 g) lean lamb or beef steak in one piece

6 tablespoons ghee or vegetable oil

2 teaspoons garlic purée

2 teaspoons ginger purée

10 green cardamom pods, seeds extracted

7 fl oz (200 ml) milk

8 tablespoons onion purée

1 tablespoon garam masala

1 teaspoon ground mace

5 fl oz (150 ml) single cream

2 tablespoons ground almonds

1 tablespoon white sugar

salt to taste

1 Ask the butcher for lamb steak. It is a fatless top of leg piece which can be beaten. If this is unavailable use good quality beef steak. Slice the meat into four then beat it to about $\frac{1}{4}$ inch (6 mm) thick. Halve each so that you have 8 pieces.

2 Heat the ghee or oil and stir-fry the garlic purée for 1 minute and then the ginger purée for 1 minute.

3 Add the cardamom seeds to the pan with the meat. Stir-fry to 'seal' for 2 minutes per side. Add half the milk, and lower the heat to simmer.

4 After 10 minutes or so, add the onion purée, the garam masala and mace. Stir-fry until it commences simmering, then add the remaining milk. Simmer on, stirring occasionally, for a further 10 minutes. What you are aiming to do is to soften the meat by gentle simmering in liquid – not *boiling* – so you must not allow the liquid to reduce too much, nor must there be too much. By the end of this stage, the meat should be becoming tender and it should not be dry.

5 Add the cream, almonds and sugar, and simmer until the meat is completely tender. Keep the liquid balance correct. Add salt to taste.

Serves: 4

Right
A Selection of Starters: *Shashlik Kebabs* **(page 56),** *Tandoori Sardines* **(page 61),** *Nargissi Kofta* **(page 55),** *Prawn Butterflies* **(page 60).**

ACHAR GOSHT
Meat Cooked in Pickle

I first came across this recipe in Nepal where the severe winters call for resourceful methods of drying meat and vegetables and producing fantastic pickles in the brief but hot summer. With readily available supplies of meat (gosht) in the West, this recipe uses tender cuts of lamb, beef or pork simmered with brinjal (aubergine) pickle, chutney and, if available, fresh mango slices to give a curry with a rich, sweet, sour and savoury taste. It is a speciality dish at the **Raj Tandoori**, *52 Cowcross Street, Farringdon, London, EC1.*

$1\frac{1}{2}$ lb (675 g) lean lamb, cubed

4 tablespoons ghee or vegetable oil

1 recipe portion curry masala gravy

2 tablespoons curry paste

4 tablespoons brinjal (aubergine) pickle, chopped

akhni stock or water

1 fresh mango, cut into strips

2 tablespoons chopped fresh coriander leaves

salt to taste

1 Trim the meat of any fat, gristle etc., and preheat the oven to 375°F/190°C/Gas 5.

2 Heat the oil in a casserole, and stir-fry the curry masala gravy for 3 minutes, then the paste for 3 minutes. Add the brinjal pickle and the meat. Stir around, then place in the preheated oven.

3 After 20 minutes, inspect, stir and taste. Add akhni stock or water if required. Return to the oven.

4 After 20 minutes, check again. This time add the fresh mango if available, coriander and salt to taste. Turn off the heat but leave the casserole in the oven to reach ultimate tenderness and absorb the flavours.

Note Alternatively, stir-fry on top of the stove for 45 minutes or until tender.

Serves: 4

Left
Four Favourite Restaurant Curries: (anti-clockwise) *Lamb Korma* (pages 68–9), *Medium Curry* (page 33), *Chicken Tikka Masala* (pages 104–5), *Madras Curry* (page 34).

RHOGAN JOSH GOSHT
Aromatic Lamb

Another Moghul dish, using whole aromatic spices, it is very fragrant when cooked in the correct traditional manner. Many curry houses simply make a standard medium hot curry to which they add capsicum peppers, onion and tomato. Pepper and heat should play no part in roghan, and it is sometimes referred to as a Kashmiri dish. No doubt the emperors partook of it there, and wherever they happened to be, but its true origin appears to be Iran. Rhogan josh, I am reliably informed, means 'boiled in ghee' in Persian. It is dark in colour and traditionally this was exaggerated to a dark red by use of ratin jot *(alkanet root) which, when fried, gives the ghee a deep beetroot colour, leading to one interpretation that it means cooked in red juices.*

In the Kashmiri language it means red meat and the wazas, *the feast cooks, use a purplish red flower called 'cockscomb' which grows in the spring, is dried and powdered and sprinkled into the cooking. In this recipe I have used beetroot powder to achieve the effect of cockscomb.*

This recipe is from one of Britain's top restaurants, the **Mandalay,** *8 Harrison Street, Leeds, West Yorkshire. It is a traditional Kashmiri recipe, using no garlic, ginger, onion or spurious vegetables; it does not have a long marinating time; yoghurt is used to create a gravy; and the method brings out the fragrance of the spices.*

6 tablespoons ghee or vegetable oil

1½ lb (675 g) lean lamb, cubed

5 oz (150 g) natural yoghurt

akhni stock or water

1 tablespoon fresh coriander leaves

salt to taste

Spices 1 (whole)

2 brown cardamoms

6 green or white cardamoms

4 inch (10 cm) piece cassia bark

4 bay leaves

6 cloves

1 teaspoon fennel seeds

Spices 2 (ground)

1 tablespoon garam masala

1 tablespoon beetroot powder (optional)

½ teaspoon asafoetida

½–2 teaspoons chilli powder

1 tablespoon ground white poppy seeds

1 teaspoon ground cassia

1 Heat the oil in a casserole and fry **Spices 1** for 1 minute. Add the meat and 'seal' it, stir-frying for 5 minutes. Add the yoghurt, mix in well, and place in a preheated oven at 375°F/190°C/Gas 5.

2 Inspect, stir and taste after 20 minutes. Add a little akhni stock or water if it needs it.

3 Ditto after a further 20 minutes. This time put in **Spices 2**, the fresh coriander, and salt to taste. Return to the oven. Turn off the heat, but leave the casserole in the oven to allow the meat to become completely tender and absorb all the flavours.

4 Spoon off all excess oil (keep for future use) before serving.

Note Alternatively stir-fry on stove for 45 minutes or until tender.

Serves: 4

PODINA GOSHT
Lamb Cooked with Mint

Another aromatic dish, with the mint giving a remarkable sweetness and lightness. Rarely found in the average restaurant, although quite common in the Indian home, this dish is one of the specialities at one of my top 30 restaurants, **Palash Restaurant,** *124 Kingston Road, Portsmouth, Hants.*

Follow the recipe for Methi Gosht (*pages 72–3*), but use either 3 tablespoons dried mint or 6 tablespoons fresh spearmint, (or a combination) de-stalked and chopped in place of the fenugreek.

Serves: 4

LAMB KORMA
Lamb in mild creamy sauce

The korma was created for the Moghuls. It was said that if a chef could cook a korma he could cook for the court. If he could cook two dozen variations he would be 'king of the kitchens', and cook only for the Emperor's table. One cook, it is said, had a repertoire of 365 kormas — one for every day of the year. Be that as it may, the Emperor's personal cook held a position of enormous power and influence at court. One can picture the extraordinary dishes that must have issued forth from those royal kitchens. Indeed, at the deserted city of Fatehphur Sikri near Jaipur, the kitchen building stands perfectly preserved. It was simply abandoned along with the rest of Emperor Akbar's great new walled city when the water supply ran dry in 1600, just 14 years after it was built.

With its gentle use of fragrant and aromatic whole spices and its garlic, ginger and creamy sauce, korma is perfect for the person who claims to dislike curry. No-one could possibly fail to fall in love with the korma.

But a korma must be cooked in the traditional manner. This excellent recipe is from the **Khyber** *restaurant, 44 Mayflower Street, Plymouth, Devon, and I'm sure you'll agree it is most certainly fit for the table of an emperor. It is finished off with a tarka — a fried mixture.*

$1\frac{1}{2}$ lb (675 g) fatless, boned lamb, cubed

5 oz (150 g) butter ghee or vegetable oil

2 tablespoons garlic purée

1 tablespoon ginger purée

8 tablespoons onion purée

2 teaspoons sugar

1 teaspoon salt

8 oz (225 g) natural yoghurt

6 fl oz (175 ml) single cream

akhni stock or water

Spices 1 (whole)

6 inch (15 cm) cinnamon stick

12 green cardamoms

10 cloves

8 bay leaves

1 teaspoon fennel seeds

Spices 2 (ground)

1 teaspoon cummin

2 teaspoons coriander

2 teaspoons mild curry powder

Tarka (additional spicing)

3 tablespoons ghee

$\frac{1}{3}$ teaspoon fenugreek seeds

$\frac{1}{2}$ teaspoon cummin seeds

3 tablespoons finely chopped onion

Garnish

1 dessertspoon flaked almonds

1   Trim the meat of any gristle etc, and preheat the oven to 375°F/190°C/Gas 5.

2   Heat the ghee or oil then fry **Spices 1** for 1 minute, add the garlic purée and fry for 1 minute, the ginger purée for 1 minute and the onion purée for 3 minutes. Add the sugar and salt.

3   Whilst this is frying, make a paste of **Spices 2** and a little water, then stir-fry it into the purée mixture for a final couple of minutes.

4   Combine this spice mixture with the lamb, place in a casserole and cook in the oven for 25 minutes.

5   Remove, inspect and stir then mix in the yoghurt and cream. Return to the oven for 20 more minutes.

6   Meanwhile, cook the tarka, the additional spicing. Heat the ghee and stir-fry the seeds for 1 minute. Add the onion and fry until golden brown.

7   Remove the casserole from the oven, inspect, then stir in the tarka and, if necessary, a commonsense amount of akhni stock or water if it looks too dry. Taste for tenderness. Judge how much more casseroling you need to reach complete tenderness. It will probably need at least 10 minutes more. It can be served straightaway, garnished with the flaked almonds, or reheated next day (some people prefer that, saying it is more marinated), or it can also be frozen.

Note Alternatively, stir-fry on top of the stove for 45 minutes, or until tender.

Serves: 4

JARDALOO SALI BOTI
Lamb Cooked with Apricot

The Parsee community fled from Iran (Persia), about 1,100 years ago to escape religious persecution. They settled eventually in Bombay, when it was nothing more than lagoons and swamps, having first been given sanctuary in Gujarat state. Parsee Food is as unique as the people themselves. Its origins are unmistakably Persian, with delightful combinations of meat, nuts and dry fruit.

The names of two of their dishes — dhansak, lamb cooked in a purée of lentils and vegetables, and patia, seafood in a sweet and sour and hot sauce — are part and parcel of the standard curry house menu, but it is rare to find an establishment which cooks them with true Parsee lightness of touch. This recipe is from the number one Indian restaurant outside the sub-continent — **The Bombay Brasserie,** *14 Courtfield Close, SW7, and it is dishes like this one cooked by their Parsee chef which make the Brasserie so exceptional. The lamb with its creamy sweet-and-sour sauce is enhanced by the apricot and nuts, and the crisp potato matchsticks (sali) set the dish off to perfection and are well worth the effort to make.*

$1\frac{1}{2}$ lb (675 g) lean lamb or other meat, cubed

3 fl oz (85 ml) any vinegar

6 tablespoons ghee or vegetable oil

2 teaspoons garlic purée

2 teaspoons ginger purée

1 Spanish onion, peeled and thinly sliced

3 tablespoons ground almonds

3 tablespoons mixed whole nuts (pistachio, hazel and almond)

1 tablespoon brown sugar or jaggery

1 tablespoon tomato purée

6–8 dried apricots, sliced

akhni stock or water

1 tablespoon chopped fresh coriander leaves

salt to taste

Spices 1 (whole)

3 teaspoons cummin seeds

6–8 brown cardamoms

1 teaspoon cloves

4 inch (10 cm) piece cassia bark

Spices 2 (ground)

2 teaspoons cummin

2 teaspoons coriander

1 teaspoon cassia

$\frac{1}{2}$ teaspoon green cardamoms

$\frac{1}{2}$ teaspoon black pepper

$\frac{1}{2}$ teaspoon ground fennel seeds

1 Trim the meat of any fat, gristle etc, and preheat the oven to 375°F/190°C/Gas 5.

2 Place the meat, vinegar and **Spices 1** into a lidded casserole, and put in the preheated oven for 20 minutes.

3 Meanwhile, heat the oil, and stir-fry the garlic purée for 1 minute, then the ginger purée for 1 minute, **Spices 2** for 1 minute and the onion for 5 minutes.

4 When the casserole comes out of the oven, add all the remaining ingredients except for the coriander and salt. Stir, add a little water or akhni stock if it needs it and return the casserole to the oven.

5 After a further 20 minutes take it out again. Inspect, stir, taste. Add the fresh coriander and salt to taste.

6 Return to the oven which can now be switched off. Serve when the meat is tender. Garnish with *sali* (see below).

Note Alternatively, stir-fry on top of the stove for 45 minutes – or until tender.

Serves: 4

METHI GOSHT
Meat with Fenugreek Leaf

Methi, *pronounced 'maytee', is fenugreek, which comes in three forms — seeds, fresh leaves and dried leaves. (Gosht, of course, means mutton, lamb or goat.) This dish comes from the Punjab, an area now part in Pakistan and part in the north of India. Punjabi cooking is very spicy and colourful, and it is familiar to us in the West because the first Indian restaurants which opened in Britain were run by Punjabis. Dishes such as keema, kofta, sag gosht, paratha, halva and the legendary tandoori originated in the Punjab. Moghul dishes such as korma, pasanda, roghan gosht, pullaos and biriani are also in the Punjabi repertoire, because the great Moghul city of Lahore was, until 1947, in the Punjab. It is for this reason that all these dishes became established on the curry house menu. The savoury, rich, creamy-textured spicy curries of the Punjab are very much to the taste of Western curry addicts.*

This dish is one of the most savoury. I find that dried methi leaf is more concentrated and easier to get than the fresh leaf, which in any case can go very bitter and black in colour if cooked too long. If you adore that savoury taste try this recipe from the very worthy **Parveen Tandoori,** *6 Theberton Street, London N1.*

1½ lb (675 g) lean lamb or stewing steak, cubed	*either* 4 tablespoons dried fenugreek leaf, ground,
4 tablespoons butter ghee or oil	*or* 6 tablespoons fresh fenugreek leaves, de-stalked and chopped (*or* a combination)
1 recipe portion curry masala gravy	salt to taste
2 tablespoons curry paste	
akhni stock or water	

1 Trim the meat of any fat, gristle etc., and preheat the oven to 375°F/190°C/Gas 5.

2 Heat the oil in a casserole, and stir-fry the curry purée for 3 minutes, then the paste for 3 more minutes. Stir in the meat, and place in the oven.

3 After 20 minutes, inspect, stir and taste. Add akhni stock or water if required. Replace in the oven.

4 Meanwhile, if using fresh methi, boil some water, blanch the leaves for 1 minute then strain.

5 After a second 20 minutes again inspect, stir and taste the casserole contents. The meat should be becoming tender by now. Add a little more water if needed, also the fenugreek and salt. Replace the casserole, turning off the oven heat. It should be ready after 10 minutes, but it can stay in the oven until you are ready to serve.

Note Alternatively, stir-fry on top of the stove for 45 minutes – or until tender.

Serves: 4

SALI

1 large potato, peeled
vegetable oil for deep-
   frying
garam masala
chilli powder (optional)
salt

1 Cut the potatoes into matchstick shapes (potato straws), and dry in a teatowel.
2 Preheat the oil in a deep fryer to 375°F/190°C (chip temperature).
3 Put the straws into the pan few by few, but quickly, to prevent them sticking together. Fry until they stop sizzling – the moisture is cooked out – and they are crisp and golden. Strain off excess oil, and let them stand for half an hour.
4 Sprinkle with the garam masala, chilli and salt.

Note There is another potato variant called *jali,* which are thinly sliced potato crisps, in fact. Make and spice them the same way. Sali and jali will keep crisp for many days in an airtight container.

MUTTON TIKKA MASALA
Meat in Tandoori Gravy

Halfway between Delhi and Kashmir, 7,000 feet up in the foothills of the Western Himalayas, lies Simla. It was created by the British in the 1830s and became their summer capital – a place to which they could retreat from the intense heat in the plains, in the same way that the Moghuls escaped the sun at Kashmir. Eventually several hill stations were built. They have in common a cool summer climate, hairpin roads to reach them, wonderful rose-filled gardens surrounding detached bungalows, churches and sporting clubs. Simla was the setting for Rudyard Kipling's Plain Tales from the Hills. *It was so British – and to this day it is a cool summer playground for wealthy Indians.*

The food eaten by the Brits of the Raj was more likely to be roast mutton and potatoes than mutton tikka masala, but this recipe has become one of the favourites at the curry house. Here is the recipe for it from North Wales' best Indian restaurant, **The Simla,** *4–5 Victoria Square, Llangollen, Clwyd and its sister in Oswestry.*

1½ lb (675 g) lean mutton or
   lamb, cubed
8 fl oz (250 ml) tandoori
   marinade

Sauce
3 tablespoons ghee or oil
4 oz (100 g) beef or lamb,
   ground or minced
3 tablespoons curry masala
   gravy
1 teaspoon white sugar
juice of 1 lemon

1 Trim the mutton well and marinate it in the tandoori marinade for a minimum of 6 hours and a maximum of 30 hours.

2 Preheat the oven to 375°F/190°C/Gas 5. Place the meat with the marinade on an oven tray and cook for 20 minutes. Baste and taste. Continue until tender (another 20 minutes at least).

3 Meanwhile, heat the ghee or oil, and fry the ground meat and curry gravy for the sauce for 20 minutes, adding water as needed to keep it from sticking. Add the sugar and lemon juice and continue to stir-fry. Add more curry gravy to achieve the texture of your choice.

4 Add the cooked meat and its liquid when cooked. Simmer to amalgamate, and then serve.

Serves: 4

MUTTON PALAK
Lamb Cooked with Spinach

Picture, if you will, a balmy evening just after the sun has set. On a lake in Udaipur a marble Maharaja's palace appears to be floating on the water in the purple-red dusk.

I will always remember that scene as I approached this palace, now the Lake Palace Hotel, by launch. My appetite was whetted by the knowledge that the royal chefs of the ex-prince of Udaipur were laying on a special banquet to be served on palace silver thalis. It was pure fairyland — and the dinner was equally magical. It was not a complicated meal — the main course consisting of just one meat dish, mutton palak, accompanied by plain rice, breads and chutneys — but it was divine, a meal to remember.

A variation of mutton palak is sag gosht, popular at all curry restaurants, and done especially well at the **Biplob**, *30 High Street, Highworth, Swindon, Wiltshire.*

1 lb (450 g) lean lamb, cubed
1 tablespoon garam masala
3 oz (75 g) natural yoghurt
12 oz (350 g) fresh spinach, washed and chopped
6 tablespoons ghee or vegetable oil
6 teaspoons garlic purée
8 tablespoons curry masala gravy

akhni stock or water
3 fl oz (85 ml) single cream
salt to taste

Spices
1 teaspoon turmeric
1 teaspoon garlic powder
1 teaspoon chilli powder
1 teaspoon whole cummin seeds
2 teaspoons curry powder

1 Marinate the lamb with the garam masala and yoghurt for 24 hours or so.

2 Blanch the spinach in boiling water, then purée it.

3 Heat the oil and stir-fry the **Spices** for 2 minutes, then the garlic purée for 2 minutes. Add the curry masala gravy and the spinach purée, and stir-fry until simmering.

4 Place all the ingredients into a lidded casserole and put into a preheated oven at 375°F/190°C/Gas 5.

5 Inspect, stir and taste after 20 minutes. Add a little water or akhni stock if needed. Continue cooking.

6 Ditto after 20 more minutes. Add cream and salt, Serve when absolutely tender.

Serves: 4

ZAFRANI KOFTA
Spiced Meatballs with Saffron

Kofta curries are yet another of the favourite Moghul dishes. Koftas (ground spicy meatballs) are easy to mould but retaining the ball shape during cooking is not always easy, as they tend to break up. I have slightly modified this recipe, therefore, to give you a foolproof method of cooking the balls by using your oven (a piece of equipment not to hand at the time of the Moghuls and still a rare sight in Indian villages).

The creamy gravy coloured with saffron combined with the aromatically spiced balls is pure Moghul and is a dish rarely encountered in UK restaurants. I collected this recipe in Agra, and it is one of the specialities of a Kashmiri kebab chef, who works at Agra's extraordinarily elegant **Moghul Sheraton Hotel**. *He can neither read nor write. He simply learned his trade from his father who was a chef, as did his father's father, and so on right back to the court of Emperor Shah Jahan. In the 1600s the capital of the empire was Agra, and Shah Jahan undertook much building, including the Taj Mahal, built as a tomb for his wife. To do all this work it was necessary to bring in skilled labour from all parts of the empire, and the town just outside the Taj is still populated by the decendants of those labourers. Favourite chefs would certainly be required too, so I see no reason to doubt that, twelve generations or so ago, one of Shah Jahan's chefs was preparing zafrani kofta in Agra. Why should his descendant not be preparing the identical dish handed down a mere twelve times in today's Indian palace — the luxury hotel?*

Meatballs

$1\frac{1}{2}$ lb (675 g) lamb leg steak, or beef

1 teaspoon garlic purée

1 tablespoon finely chopped fresh coriander leaves

$\frac{1}{2}$ teaspoon salt

Meatball spices (ground)

4 brown cardamoms

4 green cardamoms

1 teaspoon ground cassia

$\frac{1}{2}$ teaspoon salt

Gravy

3 fl oz (85 ml) vegetable oil

2 teaspoons garlic purée

2 teaspoons ginger purée

8 tablespoons onion purée

5 oz (150 g) natural yoghurt

5 fl oz (150 ml) double cream

2 tablespoons tomato purée

20 strands saffron

salt to taste

Gravy spices (ground)

2 teaspoons coriander

$\frac{1}{2}$ teaspoon turmeric

$\frac{1}{2}$ teaspoon chilli powder

1 Trim excess fat off the meat, then dice it and grind – ideally in a food processor, or three times through a hand mincer (in India it would be hand beaten).

2 Add the garlic, coriander, salt and the **Meatball spices**. Mix well with your hands, then divide into 12 equal balls.

3 Place them on an oven tray, then bake in an oven preheated to 325°F/160°C/Gas 3 for 20 minutes.

4 During this, commence the **Gravy**. Heat the oil, and fry the garlic for 1 minute, the ginger for 2 minutes, and the onion for 3 minutes. Add the **Gravy spices** and stir-fry for 2 minutes.

5 Now fold in the yoghurt and cream, tomato purée and saffron. Stir-fry until simmering.

6 Just before adding the cooked meatballs, check that there is enough liquid in the sauce. You will probably need to add some (use the liquid from the oven tray if any and/or water to get a nice texture). Add the balls and some salt. Simmer until hot, then serve.

Serves: 4

RAAN
Spicy-Coated Roast Leg of Lamb

Leg of lamb suits the tandoori process, and this recipe is one of the culinary gems from Moghul India. As with all tandoori cooking, the secret lies in marinating for at least 24 hours (48 is even better for this particular dish). The spicing is especially aromatic in this recipe, which is from India's foremost tandoori restaurant, the **Bukharra**, *located at the Welcom-Sheraton Mauyra Hotel in Delhi.*

$3\frac{1}{2}$–4 lb (1.5–1.8 kg) leg of lamb on the bone

Marinade

5 oz (150 g) natural yoghurt

2 teaspoons garlic purée

2 teaspoons ginger purée

2 tablespoons ground almonds

2 teaspoons coconut powder

1 teaspoon salt

3 fl oz (85 ml) vegetable oil

Spices

1 tablespoon tandoori paste

1 tablespoon garam masala

$\frac{1}{2}$ teaspoon ground green cardamoms

$\frac{1}{2}$ teaspoon ground fennel seeds

2 teaspoons poppy seeds

2 teaspoons dried mint

Garnish (optional)

20–30 whole almonds, roasted or fried

2 tablespoons chopped fresh coriander leaves

1 Stab the lamb all over to the bone with a sharp knife to enable the marinade to penetrate the meat.

2 In a bowl large enough to hold the meat, mix all the remaining ingredients – the marinade and the **Spices** – into a paste.

3 Put the meat into the bowl of paste, and poke the paste into all the gashes, ensuring the meat is well coated.

4 Leave in the fridge to marinate for a minimum of 6 hours, a maximum of 30. The longer you leave it, the better the paste will seep in and adhere to the meat during cooking.

5 Preheat the oven to 350°F/180°C/Gas 4 maximum, and slow-roast the lamb for about 3 hours. When really tender, the flesh should literally fall off the bone. Prior to serving, let it rest for 30 minutes or so in a low oven.

6 An optional garnish is to press roasted or fried whole almonds into the gashes then sprinkle with fresh coriander.

Serves: 4

BALTI GOSHT
Pot-Cooked Meat

Balti *is an Urdu word, and refers to a special bucket-shaped pot used for cooking in the central part of Pakistan, around Lahore. It is a traditional winter-time preparation when village families get together around a charcoal fire and cook balti gosht in the balti hanging over the charcoal fire. It is usually eaten with naan bread. In Pakistan they drink sherbat with it. This recipe is from the* **Friends Corner Restaurant***, 547 Foleshill Road, Coventry.*

either 1½ lb (675 g) leg of
  lamb, cubed,
or 2¼ lb (1 kg) lamb on the
  bone
4 garlic cloves, chopped
1 teaspoon salt
4 tablespoons vegetable oil
1 Spanish onion, peeled and
  chopped
½ red capsicum pepper,
  diced
1–4 fresh chillies, chopped
  (to taste)

2 fresh tomatoes, quartered
1 teaspoon cummin seeds,
  roasted
1 tablespoon chopped fresh
  coriander leaves

Spices
4 inch (10 cm) piece cassia
  bark
6 whole cloves
6 brown cardamoms

1 Wash the lamb, then place it in a lidded casserole or saucepan with about 12 fl oz (350 ml) water. Add the garlic, salt and **Spices.**

2 Either place in a preheated oven at 375°F/190°C/Gas 5 or on the stove, and cook, covered, until just tender (about 45 minutes). Inspect from time to time, then remove from heat and let it stand in its steam with the lid still on, for 20 minutes or so.

3 Meanwhile heat the oil in a large karahi, fry the onion until golden, then add the red pepper, chillies and tomatoes. Cook until it is nearly dry (about 10 minutes on a lowish heat).

4 Then add the drained meat to the karahi, with a little of the liquid. Stir-fry until it becomes quite dry, adding the cummin seeds and the fresh coriander about 5 minutes before it is ready.

5 The dish is served in cast-iron karahis (also called *baltis* in the Lahore area). You can serve it in any way you wish, but serving the correct way does seem to enhance it.

Serves: 4

KURZI OR KASHI
Festive Whole Lamb

The walls of Shah Jahan's magnificent Lal Qila Red Fort in Delhi are 100 feet (30 metres) high and enclose an area of 124 acres. Let into the wall are six huge arched gates, large enough to admit processional elephants. The most important entrance was the Kurzi or Khirzi gate which led directly from the fort's river frontage to the Emperor's private apartments. It was the gate through which Shah Jahan entered to inaugurate the building in 1648 and through which all important dignitaries entered the fort to attend on the Emperor. Above the Kurzi gate is an overhanging balcony contained within a domed octagonal tower at which the ruling emperor would appear each sunrise before large waiting crowds.

The most festive Indian dish is called the Kurzi or Kashi. There is one restaurant in London where you can pay £400 for a single dish. The restaurant is the **Sonar Gaon,** *46 Upper Street, London N1 and the dish is the Kashi. It is, in fact, a whole lamb baked in a mixture of spices, stuffed with basmati rice, and it serves at least 25 people.*

The kurzi dish is usually a leg of lamb about 3½ lb–4 lb (1.5–1.8 kg), to serve four. Make up about one-third quantity of the marinade, and follow the recipe, adjusting baking times according to weight. It is ordered and prepared in advance to allow the marinade to seep in. Typical is the **Bekash,** *50 High Street, Stoney Stratford, Milton Keynes, Buckinghamshire.*

This recipe from the Sonar Gaon is for a 40–45 lb (18–20 kg) lamb, but this needs a huge oven, so I have scaled it down. The smallest whole lamb you can get is Shetland baby lamb, which is available between 8–12 lb (3.6–5.4 kg). You can get the whole carcass boned and rolled so that it will easily go into your oven, and will feed 16–20 people. Alternatively you can ask for kid goat starting at 10 lb (4.5 kg). Good butchers will oblige. It makes a great talking point at a dinner party – and, quite frankly, it's really easy to cook.

1 baby whole lamb

Marinade
4 tablespoons garlic purée
6 tablespoons ginger purée
1 pint (600 ml) onion purée
5 oz (150 g) natural yoghurt
5 fl oz (150 ml) vegetable oil
2 teaspoons salt

Spices
1 teaspoon chilli powder
1 teaspoon turmeric
2 teaspoons ground coriander
2 teaspoons curry powder
1 teaspoon ground white cummin
1 tablespoon garam masala

Spices continued	*Garnish*
6 bay leaves	roasted almonds
8 brown cardamoms	mustard and cress
10 inch (25 cm) piece cassia bark	chopped fresh coriander leaves
1 teaspoon black cummin seeds	
8 cloves	

1   Mix up the marinade ingredients, including the **Spices**, and let it stand for around an hour to blend well.

2   Wash the lamb and remove any surface fat. Prick it all over with the knife point quite deeply to assist the marinade to penetrate.

3   Preheat oven to 350°F/180°C/Gas 4. While it is warming up, choose a good sized baking tray and coat the lamb with the marinade. Keep back any spare for later.

4   Roast the lamb for 1 hour then remove and baste with more marinade. Return to the oven and continue for another whole hour. Baste again. Exactly how long the process will take depends on the weight of the lamb, but allow at least 30 minutes per lb (450 g) and allow between 20–30 minutes for it to rest in a low oven before serving. But because of variations in oven temperatures or the tenderness of the meat you *must* check how things are going by inserting a knife point into the lamb during cooking. So, with the slow cooking method, a 10 lb (4.5 kg) lamb will take 5 hours to cook plus the resting time.

5   To serve, you must aim for maximum impact, so place the whole cooked lamb on a large oval serving platter. The meal will be served with a festive rice (Navrattan pullao, for example), a tasty vegetable dish and plenty of curry gravy. Garnish the lamb by placing it on a bed of rice and by liberally sprinkling it with roasted almonds, mustard and cress and fresh coriander.

Serves: 16–20

REMPAH
Malay Curry

Malaya had for centuries been a rendezvous for spice traders from China, India and Arabia before it became Moslem in 1414. The Portuguese brought Christianity and their ways to the area a century later and the Dutch and British followed. Singapore, at the tip of the thumb-shaped peninsula, was established in 1819 by Sir Stamford Raffles in the name of Britain.

All these cultural influences have left a remarkable melée of religions, languages and culinary styles. Malaysian cuisine combines the best of Indian and Chinese with a sprinkling of Thai thrown in. I obtained this recipe for Rempah Malay curry from the celebrated **Raffles Hotel** *in Singapore. Coconut, lemon grass, tamarind, five-spice powder and curry spices combine to produce an aromatic, tangy, yet creamy curry. Adjust the chilli quantity to your taste.*

$1\frac{1}{2}$ **lb (675 g) lean lamb or beef, cubed**

1 large onion, peeled and roughly chopped

6 garlic cloves

1–6 fresh chillies (to taste)

1 red capsicum pepper, seeded

2 inch (5 cm) cube fresh ginger

6 tablespoons vegetable oil or ghee

3–4 fl oz (85–120 ml) milk

$3\frac{1}{2}$ **oz (90 g) creamed coconut**

3 tablespoons desiccated coconut

2 tablespoons tamarind purée

Spices (ground)

1 teaspoon coriander

$\frac{1}{2}$ **teaspoon cummin**

$\frac{1}{2}$ **teaspoon five-spice powder**

$\frac{1}{2}$ **teaspoon garlic powder**

$\frac{1}{4}$ **teaspoon lemon grass powder**

1 teaspoon paprika

$\frac{1}{4}$ **teaspoon chilli powder**

$\frac{1}{2}$ **teaspoon turmeric**

1 teaspoon coconut powder

1 Add enough water to the **Spices** to make a stiffish paste, then leave to stand for a few minutes.

2 Make a purée of the onion, garlic, chillies, capsicum pepper and ginger.

3 Heat the oil and fry the spice paste for 5 minutes or so; stir to prevent sticking. Then add the purée and fry for 15 minutes.

4 Combine the cubed meat with the above in a casserole and place in an oven preheated to 375°F/190°C/Gas 5. Cook for about 1 hour.

5 Meanwhile heat the milk and melt the coconut block.

6 Brown the desiccated coconut under the grill.

7 Halfway through the cooking of the casserole, add the two coconuts and the tamarind purée to the dish. Stir, and add water or stock if it needs it.

Serves: 4

KEEMA PUNJABI MASALA
Punjabi Minced Curry

Minced meat is particularly good curried. Keema (mince) appears on the menus of a good many curry houses, but it is not the most popular dish, probably because it's one of those dishes most people don't bother to try. But try it you should: it is relatively inexpensive, it has a splendid texture, it cannot be overcooked – timings are not critical (so it makes a good dish for the beginner to try) – and it is very tasty. This recipe, from one of Britain's best and most attractively furnished restaurants, the **Shish Mahal***, 45 Gibson Street, Glasgow, is particularly good.*

$1\frac{1}{2}$ lb (675 g) lean lamb,
  minced

6 fl oz (175 ml) vegetable oil

4 teaspoons garlic purée

3 teaspoons ginger purée

12 tablespoons onion purée

2 tomatoes, chopped

2 tablespoons tomato purée

1 tablespoon coconut
  powder

juice of 1 lemon

1 green capsicum pepper,
  seeded and chopped

salt to taste

Spices

2 teaspoons garam masala

2 tablespoons curry powder
  or paste

1 teaspoon poppy seeds

up to 3 teaspoons chilli
  powder (to taste)

1 Heat the oil and fry the purées for, respectively, 1 minute, 2 minutes and 5 minutes.

2 Make a paste of the **Spices**, using a little water, then add and fry for 3 minutes.

3 When bubbling, add the tomatoes, tomato purée, and coconut, then add the minced lamb.

4 Place in a casserole and put into an oven preheated to 375°F/190°C/Gas 5 for 20 minutes, then check, stir and add some water if necessary.

5 Add the lemon juice, chopped pepper and salt, and continue braising for a further 20 minutes. Serve. (You could also stir-fry on the stove for the same amount of time.)

Serves: 4

MAGAZ
Brain Curry

It was the British who invented Pakistan in August 1947. It was done with some reluctance and with the best of intentions, but it caused a lot of bad feelings amongst the Hindu and Moslem communities. Moslems were the majority in north-west and north-east India – the heartlands of former Arab, Turkish, Persian and Moghul invaders – but measured over all India they represented just 10 per cent of the population. With the departure of the British Raj, the Moslems feared it would be replaced with a Hindu Raj which would persecute the Moslem minority. Partition came about in 1947, largely because of the efforts of one man, Mohammed Ali Jinna.

__Salloo's Restaurant__, 62 Kinnerton Street, London SW1, is one of the few Pakistani restaurants in Britain. Its owner, Mr Sallahuddin (Salloo himself) is from Lahore, and operates a similarly named restaurant in that city. On the restaurant's menu are traditional tasty Punjabi dishes, including this speciality.

1 lb (450 g) lamb's brain (2–
   3 brains, depending on
   the size of the lambs)
2 tablespoons any vinegar
2 tablespoons vegetable oil
6 tablespoons curry masala
   gravy
1 tablespoon chopped fresh
   coriander leaves
salt

Spices
2 teaspoons curry powder
2 teaspoons garam masala
1 teaspoon turmeric
$\frac{1}{2}$ teaspoon chilli powder

1 Mix the **Spices** with the vinegar, and let stand for a while.
2 Wash the brains then cut into bite-sized pieces. Place the pieces in a bowl with the spice paste, and enough water to cover. Stand for 1 hour.
3 Heat the oil in a karahi, and stir-fry the curry gravy for 5 minutes.
4 Add the brains with the marinade and simmer until cooked – about 20 minutes – stirring occasionally.
5 Add the coriander and salt to taste. Simmer a few minutes more, then serve.

Serves: 4

PUTTAN
Kidney curry

As the British gained more and more power in India, opposition was encountered at regular intervals. One incident in particular was blown out of all proportion. As the British turned Calcutta from swamp to city, the ruler of Bengal, the Nawab, grew envious and apprehensive. In 1756 he captured Calcutta and locked up 146 British men, women and children in a tiny room on the night of the attack. It was June, the hottest, most humid time of the year, and the lack of ventilation and the crush in the room was appalling. When the captors opened the doors next morning, all but 23 had died of suffocation. The room became known as 'The Black Hole of Calcutta', and the incident so incensed the British that they recaptured Calcutta, deposed the Nawab, and deployed high-speed cavalry troops to prevent a similar attack from happening ever again. The Bengal Lancers became the Indian Army's crack regiment.

One of London's crack restaurants is **The Bengal Lancer**, 253 Kentish Town Road, NW5, and they recently introduced this recipe to their menu.

1 lb (450 g) lamb's kidneys, trimmed, washed and cut into bite-sized pieces	8 tablespoons onion purée akhni stock or water
2 teaspoons salt	*Spices*
3–4 fl oz (85–120 ml) any vinegar	$\frac{1}{2}$ teaspoon turmeric
6 tablespoons ghee or vegetable oil	1 teaspoon ground ginger
2 teaspoons garlic purée	1 teaspoon chilli powder 2 teaspoons curry powder

1 Let the kidneys stand in a marinade of the salt and vinegar for about 1 hour.

2 Mix the **Spices** with a little water to make a paste.

3 Heat the ghee in a karahi, and stir-fry the garlic for 1 minute then the onion for 3 minutes. Add the spice paste and stir-fry for a further 3 minutes.

4 Add the kidneys and their marinade, and stir-fry to seal. Simmer for 20 minutes, adding stock or water as required.

Serves: 4

WEST INDIAN GOAT CURRY

The Spanish attempted to reach India by sailing due West. Christopher Columbus landed in the islands off America in 1492. He believed he had reached India, and the misnomer 'West Indies' has remained. Centuries later, when the West Indies came under British rule, they settled numbers of Indians there, and with them came their cooking.

West Indian goat curry is a celebrated dish. Of the several Caribbean restaurants in London, Beewees, 96 Stroud Garden, London N4, has this dish on the menu. Use goat, if you can get it, or mutton or lamb. The end result is slightly sweet, but omit the sugar if you prefer a more savoury taste. And to give the dish a really Caribbean flavour, add a tot of rum a few minutes before serving.

1¼ lb (675 g) best lamb, mutton or goat

1 large onion, peeled and chopped

4 garlic cloves, chopped

2 inch (5 cm) piece fresh ginger, chopped

4 tablespoons vegetable oil

1 green capsicum pepper, seeded

4 tomatoes

4 slices fresh or canned pineapple

1 tablespoon brown sugar salt

Spices 1 (ground)

1 teaspoon turmeric

1 teaspoon coriander

1 teaspoon cummin

2 teaspoons paprika

Spices 2 (whole)

½ teaspoon coriander seeds

3 green cardamoms

3 bay leaves

1 teaspoon black peppercorns

2 inch (5 cm) piece cassia bark

1 Cut the meat into 2 inch (5 cm) cubes, discarding unwanted fat and gristle, etc. Wash it and let it dry.

2 Fry the onion, garlic and ginger in the oil until golden.

3 Make a paste of **Spices 1** with a little water and add to the onions. Fry for a further 10 minutes, stirring continuously. Add water to keep it from sticking.

4 In a casserole combine the onion, **Spices 2**, the meat and 6–8 fl oz (175–250 ml) water. Cook in a preheated oven at 375°F/190°C/Gas 5 for 30 minutes.

5 Add the remaining ingredients and salt, stir well and cook for a further 10–15 minutes. Serve with brown rice and wedges of lemon.

Serves: 4

VENISON CURRY

Sikkim is a tiny Buddhist state in the north-east of India, its neighbours being Nepal, Tibet and Bhutan. Its original mountain people – called Lepchas – are good hunters, catching fish in the mountain streams and wild boar or wild deer, which are considered a Lepcha delicacy. Another of their favourite treats is the larvae of a particular wasp which they eat with chopsticks. I regret I do not have the recipe for this dish.

Herds of wild deer exist in certain parts of India, although they are not as prevalent as they are in Africa. Venison is now easier to come by from the city butchers of Delhi and Bombay – indeed there are large venison farms near Bombay. It is a powerfully flavoured meat, not to everyone's taste perhaps, but it curries well, although I would not try to be too subtle with spicing. Venison, by the way, was a great favourite with the Moghul emperors. This venison recipe is one of the unusual dishes served by the remarkable **Dewaniam** *restaurant, 133 Stanstead Road, London SE23.*

$1\frac{1}{2}$ lb (675 g) best quality
  venison, diced
3 tablespoons ghee or
  vegetable oil
1 tablespoon garlic purée
1 tablespoon ginger purée
8 tablespoons onion purée
1 × 14 oz (400 g) can
  tomatoes

Spices 1
1 teaspoon chilli powder
2 teaspoons ground
  coriander
1 teaspoon ground cummin
2 teaspoons paprika
1 teaspoon turmeric

Spices 2
1 tablespoon garam masala
1 tablespoon dry fenugreek
  leaf

1 Wash excess blood off the meat and trim off any unwanted pieces.

2 Heat the oil and stir-fry the garlic, ginger and onion for 1 minute, 2 minutes and 5 minutes respectively.

3 Meanwhile, open the can of tomatoes and strain. Mix the tomato juice from the can with **Spices 1** to get a runny paste, and preheat the oven to 375°F/190°C/Gas 5.

4 Add the paste to the purée mixture, stirring to prevent sticking, and fry until the water evaporates (about 5–8 minutes). When the oil floats to the top, it is done. Take off the heat and set aside.

5 In a casserole, heat the meat on the stove (at a medium-high heat) for 10–15 minutes to remove excess fluids. Strain, reserving liquid.

6 In the casserole, combine the purée-paste mixture, the meat and the tomatoes. Put into the preheated oven and cook for 40 minutes. At the start it should neither be too dry nor too runny. Check from time to time, stirring, and add sufficient reserved meat liquid to keep it creamy and fluid, not dry.

7 After 40 minutes, add **Spices 2**, stir well, and cook on for 15 or so minutes. The meat should be cooked by now, but if it is still chewy, carry on cooking until you are satisfied.

Serves: 4

SAG VENISON

Follow the above recipe but add 12 oz (350 g) spinach, either fresh – washed, chopped and blanched – or canned. Add it at stage 6 of the method and proceed with the other steps.

5

CHICKEN

We are very lucky – complacent even – with the quality of chickens we get in the West. They are great plump, succulent birds yielding plenty of meat. On the sub-continent most of the birds are scrawny and tough, probably because they scratch out a rather less well-fed existence than their factory-bred cousins in the West. This is ironic because the chicken almost certainly originated in the jungles of India some 50,000 years before people found their way there. In today's India, the chicken is a luxury item, although intensive farming is beginning to creep in around major cities.

Yet chicken is, in my view, the perfect meat for currying. It is quick to cook, tender and delicious. Always remove and discard the skin.

Turkey is an excellent substitute for chicken in any of the following recipes. However, it rarely appears on the menus of our curry restaurants, and is not part of the tradition of the curry lands.

BANGLADESH KURMA OR KORMA
Mild Chicken Curry

This mild, most aromatic dish makes an interesting comparison with the meat korma recipe on pages 64–5. Chicken breast is succulent and perfect with the aromatic spices, cream, yoghurt and nuts. The saffron strands give the dish a lovely pale yellow colour. Do not use turmeric here: the colour it gives is a little on the green side of yellow.

This recipe comes from the Bangladeshi-run **Kuti's Restaurant,** *70 London Road, Southampton. It is a sumptuous dish, ideal for dinner parties or for first-time curry diners.*

1½ lb (675 g) chicken breast, skinned and cubed

6 tablespoons butter ghee or vegetable oil

1 teaspoon ground saffron powder or yellow food colouring

4 tablespoons milk

4 teaspoons garlic purée

8 tablespoons onion purée

2 teaspoons garam masala

2½ oz (65 g) natural yoghurt

5 fl oz (150 ml) double cream

2 tablespoons ground almonds

20 saffron strands (about 1/10 of a gram!)

salt to taste

Garnish

2 tablespoons chopped fresh coriander leaves

30 whole almonds, roasted

1 Heat the ghee and mix the saffron powder or colouring with milk.

2 Heat the oil and quickly 'seal' the chicken cubes by turning frequently for 2 minutes, then add the yellow milk and stir-fry for 2 minutes.

3 Add the garlic and stir-fry for 1 minute, then the onion for around 3 minutes – enough to remove the moisture content. Now add the garam masala and stir-fry for 2 more minutes. Your total frying time is around 10 minutes, and the chicken is half cooked.

4 Add the yoghurt, cream and ground almonds and when it starts to simmer turn the heat down and stir-fry for 10 minutes more to ensure it does not stick, adding milk or water as necessary.

5 Place the saffron strands in a little warm water and extract as much colour as you can by gently mashing with a teaspoon.

6 Check that the chicken is cooked right through by cutting a large piece across. Simmer on if required. Just prior to serving add the saffron and salt to taste. Garnish with the coriander and almonds, and serve immediately.

Serves: 4

MURGH BADAM PASANDA
Chicken Pasanda with Nuts

The British were in India for just 239 years, from the first tentative visits to the courts of the Moghul emperors in 1608, until they withdrew from India in 1947. The Raj was at its height from 1757, when India came under the direct control of the British crown. Queen Victoria was proclaimed Empress of India in 1877. The great city of New Delhi was built by the architect Edward Lutyens in the 1920s to be Britain's capital of the Empire. But the sun was already setting on the Raj, and World War II was the last straw. India demanded her independence and achieved it in 1947.

The British did a lot for India. They unified the 650 princedoms and kingdoms. They created the world's greatest rail network, the judiciary system, a democracy and a highly disciplined army. They also left India with a bureaucracy as complex as can be imagined, and an English-speaking people with 15 native languages.

Despite being an occupying force, not always popular, the Raj is remembered with some respect by British and Indians alike for its elegance and high living. The first restaurant to encapsulate these memories in its name was **The Last Days of the Raj***, 22 Drury Lane, London WC2. It obtained enormous publicity when a group of eight former curry waiters and chefs obtained a bank loan guarantee from Camden Council in North London enabling them to start a cooperative venture in 1982. This recipe is one of the reasons why The Last Days is a popular restaurant.*

4 chicken breasts, boned and skinned

3 tablespoons ghee or vegetable oil

$\frac{1}{2}$ **Spanish onion, peeled and chopped**

1 teaspoon garlic purée

2 oz (50 g) cashew nuts

$\frac{1}{2}$ **teaspoon ground cloves**

$\frac{1}{4}$ **teaspoon ground green cardamoms**

2 teaspoons turmeric

1 teaspoon ground white pepper

Marinade

5 oz (150 g) natural yoghurt

1 teaspoon ginger purée

2 teaspoons ground white pepper

1 teaspoon ground cloves

1 teaspoon ground coriander

$\frac{1}{2}$ **teaspoon ground aniseed**

Garnish

toasted slivered almonds

chopped fresh coriander leaves or fresh parsley

1 Combine the marinade ingredients. Liberally brush the marinade on the chicken. Cover and refrigerate for several hours.

2 Remove the chicken from the marinade and set the latter aside for later use.

3 Sauté the chicken over medium heat in the ghee or oil until golden brown – about 3 or 4 minutes each side. Remove and set aside.

4 Fry the onion, garlic and cashews in the same pan until they are golden brown – about 2 minutes.

5 Take the pan off the heat and scrape the contents into a food processor or blender. Add the cloves, cardamom, turmeric, pepper and 2 fl oz (50 ml) water to the blender or processor. Purée into a paste.

6 Return the paste to the frying pan and simmer over medium heat for 5 minutes, stirring occasionally. Add 6–8 fl oz (175–250 ml) water and the chicken with the reserved marinade, and continue to stir-fry for a further 15–20 minutes.

7 Sprinkle with toasted almonds and the coriander or parsley before serving. Accompany dish with white rice and coconut chutney.

Serves: 4

MURGH MASALAM OR KURZI
Whole Baked Chicken

Kurzi chicken is served on special occasions (as is the lamb version on pages 80–81). Sometimes called murgh masalam, the dish requires a whole chicken which is marinated in a masala paste for up to 24 hours. It is then stuffed with spicy mincemeat and cooked.

I have in my recipe collection a book called The Cooking Delights of the Maharajas, *written by the ex-Maharaja of the state of Sailana, and it includes recipes of his own and of other royal families in India. Two of the recipes are different ways of preparing this dish. One is skewer-cooked over charcoal or in the tandoor. The other method is intriguing if a little impractical in the UK, but I feel sure you would like to know that the Maharaja recommends the stuffed chicken be placed in an earthenware pot at the bottom of which cinammon sticks are spread crosswise in such a way that the chicken shall not touch the pot. Place the chicken in. Close the pot with the lid. Prepare a thick paste of black beans, flour and water. Seal the edges of the lid with the paste. Dig a round pit 18 inches (45 cm) deep and 18 inches (45 cm) wide in dry ground, light 20 cow-dung cakes and let them burn until white ash appears. Then put some in the pit. Put the pot in and put the remaining burning dung around and on top of it. Remove after 2 hours, and serve. I would dearly like to try this age-old authentic method!*

Meanwhile, with sincere thanks to Maharaja Diguijaya Singh, here is a modified version of this fabulous dish. I have given quantities for four as usual, but it can easily be stepped up using a larger chicken. For a really splendid occasion use a turkey. A 10 lb (4.5 kg) turkey will serve 12.

Many UK restaurants serve kurzi chicken or murgh masalam. A very good recipe comes from the **Manzil**, *67 Grange Road East, Birkenhead, Merseyside.*

1 roasting chicken about 3½ lb (1.5 kg)
ghee or vegetable oil for basting

Marinade

1 teaspoon turmeric
2 tablespoons ground coriander
2 teaspoons garam masala
2 teaspoons salt
8 tablespoons onion purée
4 tablespoons curry paste

Filling

8 oz (225 g) sheek kebab mince, uncooked (page 53)
2–4 whole potatoes, peeled

1 Skin the chicken, wash and dry it.

2 Make up the marinade and thoroughly coat the chicken in it. Leave for 6 hours.

3 When you want to cook the chicken, preheat the oven to 375°F/190°C/Gas 5.

4 Stuff the mince into the chicken cavity, filling the remaining space with the whole raw potatoes.

5 Place the chicken on a rack on an oven tray and bake for 20 minutes per lb (450 g). Baste every 15 minutes with ghee. On the hour for a $3\frac{1}{2}$ lb (1.5 kg) bird, increase the heat to 425°F/220°C/Gas 7, and give it a final 10 minutes at that heat.

6 Remove the chicken from the oven, place in a low oven and let it rest for about 15 minutes before serving.

Serves: 4

CHICKEN DHANSAK
Chicken Cooked with Lentils and Vegetables

The authentic dhansak is a Parsee dish. Mutton is slowly cooked with lentils and vegetables, and it is one of the best loved dishes, regarded as a Sunday lunch special in the way we regard a roast. This recipe is a curry house standard and to prove it, I received virtually identical recipes from four restaurants across the nation: the **Ashoka**, *365 Lisburn Road, Belfast, N. Ireland; the* **Shish Mahal**, *68 Union Street, Aberdeen; the* **Asia**, *90 Fisherton Street, Salisbury, Wiltshire; and the* **Taj Mahal**, *77 Leigh Road, Leigh, Essex.*

You can use meat, seafood or vegetables for this recipe. Simply adjust timings up or down as needed. The Parsees would traditionally serve brown rice with dhansak.

1 lb (450 g) chicken breast, skinned and cubed

4 oz (105 g) red lentils (masoor dhal)

4 tablespoons vegetable oil

1 teaspoon turmeric

8 tablespoons curry masala gravy

2 tablespoons curry paste

Akhni stock or water

1–2 pieces canned pineapple, drained and chopped

14 oz (400 g) mixed vegetables, diced (carrot, potato, peas, aubergine, beans, okra, tomato, capsicum: or canned ratatouille)

1 tablespoon sugar

salt to taste

1 tablespoon garam masala

1 Sift through the lentils and rinse them, then cook by boiling in an equal volume of water, about 3–4 fl oz (85–120 ml). They will be cooked sufficiently in about 30 minutes.

2 Meanwhile, heat the oil in a karahi, stir-fry the turmeric for a few seconds then add a spoonful of curry gravy. Take a quarter of the chicken and stir-fry it, sealing it and colouring it yellow. Add more gravy, the next quarter of chicken and so on until all the gravy and chicken are used. Add the paste and a little stock or water.

3 Simmer for about 10 minutes then check to see whether the chicken is cooked. When it is, combine with the remaining ingredients, and mix well. When simmering it is ready to serve.

Serves: 4

Right
Four Unusual Curries: *Pili-Pili Chicken* (**page 103**), *Rhogan Josh Gosht* (**pages 66–7**), *Sri-Lankan Duck* (**page 113**), *Machher Jhol* (**page 118**).

BHOONA CHICKEN
Dry Stir-Fried Chicken

This is a simple dish to make using stir-fry techniques. The cooking takes 20 minutes, the preparation no more than 5 — less time than it takes to heat up a frozen meal. Quickly prepare a rice dish and you have instant curry and rice.

This recipe is from a restaurant in the north-east of Britain which is fast establishing a good reputation — the **Dilshad Tandoori**, *49 Church Street, Hartlepool, Cleveland.*

1½ lb (675 g) chicken breast, skinned and cubed

2 tablespoons ghee or vegetable oil

1 teaspoon turmeric

8 tablespoons curry masala gravy

2 tablespoons chopped fresh coriander leaves

2 tablespoons natural yoghurt

Spices 1 (whole)

4 bay leaves

6 small pieces cassia bark

6 cloves

Spices 2 (ground)

1 tablespoon garam masala

0–2 teaspoons chilli powder (to taste)

1 Heat the oil and fry **Spices 1** for 1 minute.

2 Add the chicken with the turmeric, and stir-fry for 5 minutes. Then add a spoonful of gravy, stir until it is absorbed, about 2 minutes, then add more. Repeat this process until the gravy is all in. The chicken should be fairly dry and nearly cooked after about 15 minutes.

3 Now add **Spices 2**, the fresh coriander and the yoghurt. Stir-fry a further 2–3 minutes and serve.

Serves: 4

Left
Some Exotic Dishes: *Stuffed Baked Glazed Quail* (pages 108–9), *Noor Mahal Biriani* (pages 157–9), *Anarkali Bahar/Sizzling Tandoori Chicken* (page 106).

CHICKEN JALFREZI

Liphook is renowned for a very good restaurant — the **Lal Quilla***, 15 The Square, Liphook, Hampshire. Its name means 'Red Fort' and it refers to the great edifice in Delhi, constructed in 1638 by the Emperor Shah Jahan. It was the seat of empire for 200 years and much of it stands today, stripped of its wealth perhaps, but not its majesty. The greatest ravage at the Red Fort took place in 1739 when a Turkish invader massacred 50,000 citizens. His object was to take as much treasure as he could, and his success can be measured by the fact that it needed 1,000 captured elephants, 5,000 camels and 10,000 horses to carry his booty off to his homelands (including Shah Jahan's astounding gold 'peacock throne', encrusted with hundreds of huge diamonds, pearls, sapphires, rubies and emeralds).*

This dish too is a jewel. It is colourful and incredibly simple to make, taking just 20 minutes. It not only tastes fresh but the chicken takes on a golden glow from the turmeric and it is highlighted by the greens and reds of the capsicums. You'll find it on the menus of many restaurants up and down the country, but this is the Lal Quilla's version.

$1\frac{1}{2}$ **lb (675 g) chicken breast, boned and skinned**

4 tablespoons ghee or vegetable oil

2 teaspoons white cummin seeds

4 garlic cloves, finely chopped

2 inch (5 cm) piece fresh ginger, finely chopped

1 large Spanish onion, peeled and chopped

2 green chillies (or more to taste), finely chopped

$\frac{1}{2}$ **each of green and red capsicum peppers, seeded and coarsely chopped**

2 tablespoons chopped fresh coriander leaves

2 or 3 fresh tomatoes, chopped

salt to taste

lemon juice

Spices

1 teaspoon paprika

$\frac{1}{2}$ **teaspoon turmeric**

2 teaspoons curry powder

1 Cut the chicken into bite-sized pieces.

2 Heat the oil and fry the cummin seeds for 1 minute. Add the garlic and fry for 1 minute, then add the ginger and fry for a further minute.

3 Add the chicken pieces and stir-fry for about 10 minutes. The chicken should look white and nearly cooked. Lift the chicken out with a slotted spoon and put to one side.

4 Heat the remaining juices on the stove, and when hot fry the **Spices** for 3 minutes. Add the onion and chillies and continue to fry for 5 more minutes.

5 Add the peppers and fry. When they are soft, replace the chicken, add the coriander and tomatoes, and stir-fry for about 5 minutes on medium heat. Add a little water if needed.

6 Test that the chicken is cooked with a sharp knife. Add salt to taste, and serve. It's nice with a squeeze of lemon juice over the top.

NOTE: In place of the **Spices**, you can substitute 2 teaspoons of any type of curry paste.

Serves: 4

MUROG DE GAMA
Chicken de Gama

The Portuguese were the first Europeans to invade India. Navigator Vasco da Gama landed in the south in 1498, seeking both converts to Christianity and spices. The latter he found in an unexpected way – he located one of the Arab spice exchange ports. At the time, the newly founded Moghul empire, under Babur, was busy establishing itself in the north and this gave the Portuguese their foothold further south in Goa, where they established their 'capital'.

*This recipe is in memory of the Portuguese arrival in Goa and it is from an excellent and very unusual restaurant, the **India**, Rendezvous Street, Folkestone, Kent – unusual because its Indian owner/chef was trained in France, and excellent because his dishes combine French and Indian techniques as in this floured chicken dish.*

1 spring chicken, about $2\frac{1}{2}$–3 lb (1.1–1.3 kg)

3 tablespoons distilled vinegar

$1\frac{1}{2}$ teaspoons salt

$\frac{1}{2}$ teaspoon freshly ground black pepper

2 fl oz (50 ml) tamarind purée

plain flour for coating

4 tablespoons mustard oil or vegetable oil

$2\frac{1}{2}$ tablespoons finely chopped garlic

$1\frac{1}{2}$ tablespoons finely chopped ginger

4 oz (100 g) onion, peeled and finely chopped

sugar to taste

akhni stock or water

1 tablespoon finely chopped fresh coriander leaves

Spices

2 inch (5 cm) cinnamon stick, coarsely ground, *or* 2 teaspoons ground cinnamon

2 dried hot chillies, *or* $\frac{1}{4}$ teaspoon cayenne pepper

6 whole cloves

$1\frac{1}{2}$ tablespoons freshly ground coriander

2 teaspoons freshly ground cummin

$\frac{1}{2}$ teaspoon black peppercorns

2 teaspoons turmeric

1 Cut the chicken into 4 pieces (or 8 if you wish), skin it and wash in cold water. Dry well with a teatowel, put the pieces in a deep bowl and sprinkle them with vinegar, 1 teaspoon salt and the ground pepper, turning the pieces of meat over to coat them evenly. Pour the tamarind purée over the chicken, mix, and leave to marinate at room temperature for about 2 hours.

2 Drain the marinade from the chicken into the jar of an electric blender. Coat each piece of chicken with some flour so that it doesn't stick at the bottom of the frying pan.

3 Heat the oil in a large flat frying pan, and drop the chicken pieces in one by one. Turn them over frequently to brown them, and then transfer to a bowl. While frying, make sure that the heat is moderate or medium to low.

4 Add the garlic to the oil remaining in the pan and cook for 30 seconds, then add the ginger and cook for 30 seconds. Add the **Spices** and cook for 30 seconds, then the onions and $\frac{1}{2}$ teaspoon salt. Mix well and stir-fry for about 5 minutes. Add a little akhni stock or water as needed.

5 After 5 minutes, take the pan off the heat and with a spatula pour the mixture from the pan into the blender. Blend it well at high speed for about 1 minute.

6 Put the pan back on the heat, and pour in the blended mixture along with the pieces of chicken. Increase the heat and bring it to the boil, adding stock as required, and then reduce the heat to medium to low. Taste the sauce and if you find that it is a bit sour, add 2 teaspoons sugar or as necessary. Add salt to taste.

7 Simmer for 15 minutes and before switching off the heat, sprinkle the chopped coriander over the curry and leave it, covered, for about 5 minutes before serving.

Serves: 4

MURCH NAWABI
Chicken Cooked with Cream and Almonds

Lucknow is a Moslem city between Delhi and Bengal. It principally came to fame after the Moghuls departed, when it fell into the hands of an infamous succession of ten debauched, overweight Nawab-Wazirs; they reigned from the 1750s for a century in a haze of good living. Their harems and courtesan dancing girls are legendary. The final Nawab indulged himself to such excess that the British deposed him in 1856 — a factor contributing to the Mutiny of 1857.

My own family was nearly wiped out in the uprising. My great-great-grandfather and his wife were massacred along with 2,000 other British citizens. Their three-year-old daughter, Alice — my great-grandmother — was orphaned, and with no immediate family to go to was sent to the military school at Sanawar. She stayed there for nearly 15 years until Alexander Lemmon, an official at the Government Telegraph department, went to the orphanage and chose her as his bride.

I'll never know whether my family ever tasted the following recipe, a particular delicacy of the Nawabs. You'll find this dish at the aptly named **Nawab Brasserie***, 37 High Street, Harrow-on-the-Hill, Middlesex.*

1½ lb (675 g) chicken breast, skinned and cubed	1 tablespoon pistachio nuts
6 tablespoons vegetable oil or butter ghee	2 tablespoons almonds
2 teaspoons garlic purée	1 tablespoon sultanas
8 tablespoons onion purée	2 teaspoons ground cassia bark
2 tablespoons curry paste	2 tablespoons chopped fresh coriander leaves
akhni stock or water	4 eggs (optional)
5 fl oz (150 ml) single cream	

1 Heat the oil in a karahi, and stir-fry the garlic purée for 1 minute, then the onion purée for 3–4 minutes. Add the curry paste and stir-fry for another minute.

2 Add the chicken and stir-fry for 10 minutes. Use a little akhni stock or water as necessary to keep it from sticking.

3 Carefully add the cream, nuts and sultanas, the ground cassia bark and the fresh coriander.

4 Simmer for at least 10 more minutes then serve. If you like, you can garnish each helping of this dish with a fried egg.

Serves: 4

PILI-PILI CHICKEN
Chilli Chicken

The origins of this dish go back to the Moors – the Arabs who by 900 AD were in control of a gigantic empire stretching from Spain to India. They used pepper to 'heat' their food, but it was not until the Spanish discovered the New World in the sixteenth century that the chilli became an integral part of the food of the Middle East, the Orient and, of course, India.

The common misconception about curry is that it is infested with chilli to incendiary level, so it is quite remarkable to find that the chilli arrived late on in the evolution of Indian cooking. Chilli heat must be taken in moderation by those not used to it. So, this dish is not for the uninitiated. Adjust the chilli level up or down to your taste, but do not omit it altogether. You'll find chilli chicken in many restaurants. But at one, whose name (according to its owners) was carefully chosen, **The Curry Fever***, 239 Belgrave Road, Leicester, the dish is an Indo-Kenyan version and it is a fabulous, quickly made stir-fry for heat lovers. It is also on the menu of Kenya's top Indian restaurant, the* **Safeer***, Nairobi.*

$1\frac{1}{2}$ lb (675 g) chicken breast, skinned and cubed

4 tablespoons vegetable oil

2 garlic cloves, chopped

2 inch (5 cm) piece fresh ginger, chopped

$\frac{1}{2}$ Spanish onion, peeled and chopped

$\frac{1}{2}$ each of red, green and yellow capsicum peppers, chopped

3–6 fresh green chillies, chopped (to taste)

2 tablespoons chopped fresh coriander leaves

2 fresh tomatoes, chopped

salt to taste

Spices 1 (whole)

1 teaspoon white cummin seeds

1 teaspoon mustard seeds

Spices 2 (ground)

1 teaspoon turmeric

1 tablespoon curry powder

1 Heat the oil and fry **Spices 1**, the garlic, ginger and onion for just 1 minute each.

2 Add **Spices 2** and a tiny bit of water just to prevent sticking. Add the pepper, chilli and the chicken, and stir-fry for 10 minutes.

3 Add the coriander and tomatoes, and stir-fry for a minimum of 5 minutes more. Check that the chicken is cooked right through (cut a large piece in half) and if so serve at once. This dish loses freshness if it stands around.

***Serves:* 4**

CHICKEN TIKKA MASALA or REZALA
Chicken Pieces in Tandoori Sauce

I use three methods for achieving tandoori/tikkas. Firstly for small quantities I use the grill, secondly for large quantities I use the oven, and I have recently been experimenting with a third method, stir-frying, which is easier to control than the grill – the chicken cooks more evenly and does not burn so easily. My method of stir-frying also imparts a rich colour at the same time as sealing the chicken, and if you want to blacken the edges (it does add a little to the effect and taste) at the end of the stir-fry phase, just heat under the grill for a few seconds.

Putting tandoori-cooked items into a rich red tomato sauce which uses spare tandoori marinade is a relatively recent restaurateur's invention, and it has become the diners' favourite dish. The dish is encountered under several names – tikka masala, tandoori masala, tandoori or tikka makhani (butter) or makhanwalla (cooked in butter) or choosa masala or rezala. Indeed some restaurants offer most of their curries combined with the tandoori/tikka sauce so you get bhoona tikka masala or pasanda tikka masala, etc.

This recipe is an amalgam of those from several restaurants, in particular the **Oakham Tandoori***, 18 Mill Street, Leicester, the* **Dilruba***, 155 Railway Terrace, Rugby, where they call the dish rezala, and one from Wales, the* **Koh-i-noor***, Chepstow Road, Newport, Gwent.*

Tikka/tandoori

either **1½ lb (675 g) chicken breast, skinned and cubed,** *or* **a 2½–3 lb (1.1–1.3 kg) spring chicken, skinned and quartered**

juice of 2 lemons (or PLJ)

8 fl oz (250 ml) tandoori marinade

The Sauce

6 tablespoons vegetable oil

6 tablespoons curry masala gravy

2 teaspoons tandoori paste

2 tablespoons tandoori marinade

2 teaspoons tomato purée

½ green capsicum pepper, seeded and chopped

1–4 fresh green chillies, chopped (to taste)

1 tomato, chopped

2 tablespoons natural yoghurt

2 tablespoons chopped fresh coriander leaves (or purée)

1 tablespoon ground almonds

1 tablespoon single cream

1 teaspoon sugar (optional)

salt to taste

1 In the case of the quartered chicken, cut short, shallow slashes on the flesh. This gives an interesting appearance to the finished dish, and a greater surface area for the marinade to adhere to.

2 Rub the flesh with the lemon juice and let stand for 15 minutes. This degreases and tenderises the meat, preparing it for the marinade.

3 Shake off excess lemon juice (reserve any left, to use later in the sauce) and, using a deep bowl, thoroughly coat the chicken flesh with the tandoori marinade. Ensure the marinade reaches all parts generously. Leave to stand overnight, but preferably for 24 or even 30 hours – a minimum of 6 hours. The longer you leave it the deeper the marinade penetrates (but for the instant method see below).

4 *Cooking the Chicken*

To cook in the *tandoor* or over a barbecue, place the pieces or quarters on skewers. Place the skewers over the coals. Cook for 15 minutes, turning once or twice. Test for when ready, then remove.

To grill, arrange the pieces on a grill rack and place the pan about 6 inches (15 cm) below the heat which should be at three-quarters full. Cook as above.

To bake, place the pieces on an oven tray – don't cram them together, or they won't cook evenly. Place in an oven preheated to 325°F/160°C/Gas 3, and cook for 15–20 minutes.

An instant stir-frying – for *tikka* only – has worked for me very satisfactorily when I forgot to do even a 6-hour marinating. (It also works – better flavour – after a 30-hour marinating.) Simply coat the tikkas in the marinade. Heat some oil in the karahi, and stir-fry with about 4 tablespoons of excess marinade. Place the tikkas in the karahi and stir-fry for 15 minutes.

5 For the sauce, heat the oil in a karahi, and simmer the gravy, paste, marinade and purée. After 2–3 minutes add the peppers, chillies and tomato, and continue to simmer for 5 minutes or so.

6 Add all the remaining ingredients, and mix. When simmering, add the chicken, and stir through. Serve when hot.

Serves: 4

ANARKALI BAHAR
Sizzling Tandoori Chicken

The chicken pieces are tandoori marinated and baked, then they're dry-fried and brought sizzling to the table. This is a speciality dish from the **Ameena** *restaurant, 25 The Precinct, Halesowen, West Midlands. To achieve the smoky sizzle you need cast-iron sizzler platters or karahis. If you don't have these, simply serve non-sizzling. It will still taste the same.*

1½ lb (675 g) chicken breast, skinned and boned

1 Spanish onion, peeled and chopped

1 green pepper, seeded and chopped

2 tomatoes, chopped

vegetable oil

2 limes

Marinade

2 teaspoons garlic purée

1 teaspoon ginger purée

5 oz (150 g) natural yoghurt

3 tablespoons mustard oil

1 teaspoon any vinegar

juice of 1 lemon

salt to taste

Spices

1 teaspoon dried mint

2 teaspoons dry fenugreek leaf

1 tablespoon curry paste

1 tablespoon tandoori paste

2 tablespoons chopped fresh coriander leaves

1 Cube the chicken breast, and mix together the marinade ingredients and **Spices**. Combine, and leave for a minimum of 6 hours, a maximum of 30 hours in the fridge.

2 Bake the chicken pieces on a skewer over charcoal, under a grill at medium heat, or bake in the oven at 325°F/160°C/Gas 3 for 15–20 minutes. You could also stir-fry them.

3 Meanwhile take four cast-iron karahis (baltis in the Midlands) and heat them on the stove. In them stir-fry the onion, pepper and tomato in a little oil.

4 Divide the chicken between the karahis and mix. Just prior to serving, squeeze some lime juice on the karahis which, providing they're hot enough, will sizzle and give off a lot of smoke. Using tongs, serve at once.

Serves: 4

KAENG KEO WAN GAI
Thai Green Chicken Curry

*Thai curry should have that distinctive fragrance which comes from lime leaves (makrut) and lemon grass (takrai), coupled with the background tastes of shrimp paste (kapi) and fish sauce (nam-pla). The curry becomes more distinctive with the use of khaa or galingale, which I have specified in the recipe below for use in its fresh root form; if unobtainable, use a mixture of fresh ginger (to which it is related) and galingale powder. This recipe is from Britain's highly acclaimed Thai restaurant, **The Blue Elephant**, 4 Fulham Broadway, London SW6. It has a branch in Brussels and one in Bangkok.*

$1\frac{1}{2}$ lb (675 g) chicken breast, skinned, boned and diced

4 tablespoons vegetable oil

14 oz (400 ml) thick coconut milk

3 tablespoons *nam-pla* (fish sauce)

2 tablespoons sugar

2 oz (50 g) large aubergine slices (*makua paw*)

1 oz (25 g) baby aubergine (*makua puang*)

$\frac{1}{2}$ green capsicum pepper, seeded and thinly sliced

sprig of basil leaves

1 large fresh lime leaf, finely chopped

Curry paste

$1\frac{1}{2}$ green capsicum peppers, seeded and coarsely chopped

2–7 green chillies, chopped (to taste)

1 inch (2.5 cm) piece fresh galingale (*kha*) or $\frac{1}{2}$ teaspoon powder

8 tablespoons onion purée *or* finely chopped shallots

2 tablespoons garlic purée

1 teaspoon ground coriander

1 tablespoon fresh lemon grass leaves, finely chopped, *or* 1 teaspoon powder

1 tablespoon *nam-pla* (fish sauce)

1 teaspoon *kapi* (shrimp paste)

1 teaspoon chopped fresh coriander leaves

6–7 fresh or dried lime leaves

1 Blend all the curry paste ingredients in the blender or food processor to a thick paste.

2 Heat the oil in a large pan, and stir-fry the curry paste with a little coconut milk for about 5 minutes. Add the chicken pieces and stir-fry for about 10 minutes.

3 Add the remaining coconut milk, the fish sauce, sugar and aubergines, plus some water if necessary to enable the items to boil.

4 Simmer for 5 minutes then add the green pepper, basil and lime leaf. Stir in and serve promptly.

Serves: 4

STUFFED BAKED GLAZED QUAIL

Quails are quite common in northern India, where quail recipes are especially beloved by the ex-Maharajas. A few restaurants offer quail dishes in this country — either tandoori baked or curried.

This recipe is an invention of mine, combining several Indian concepts. You need boned quail — your butcher can get them boned, or you can do it yourself, but it's fiddly. The boned quails are then marinated tandoori-style for 24 hours. After being stuffed, they are baked in the oven. glazed and finished under the grill. They can be served with salad and make a fine starter or main dish.

4 boned, prepared quail (keep the skin on)

Marinade (well mixed)
3–4 oz (75–100 g) natural yoghurt
3 teaspoons tandoori paste
1 teaspoon dried mint
1 teaspoon garlic powder

Stuffing
4–6 tablespoons cooked rice

Glaze
4 tablespoons clear honey
2 teaspoons Worcestershire sauce

1 Put the quail and the marinade together in a non-metal bowl with lid. Use your fingers to ensure thorough blending. Place in the fridge for 24 hours.

2 The next day, preheat the oven to 375°F/190°C/Gas 5, and remove the quails from the marinade. Open them out and spread them on a work surface.

3 Mix into your cooked cold rice — better slightly glutinous — a small amount of spare marinade. Take about 1–1$\frac{1}{2}$ tablespoons rice, compress it, and gently fold the quail around it so that it resumes its boned shape. Tuck the flaps of skin and the legs in and gently squeeze them into shape. Place them top-side up on an oven tray. They don't need trussing providing you have got a firm shapely quail. Pour any remaining marinade over each quail.

4 Place the oven tray in the oven, and bake for 15 minutes.

5 About 4 minutes before taking them out of the oven, preheat the grill and a burner on the stove. Mix the honey and Worcestershire sauce in a small pan and heat.

6 Take the quails from the oven, and pour the glaze carefully over them, ensuring it covers all the exposed flesh.

7 Place under the grill for a minute or two to finish off. Serve hot or cold.

NOTE A more elaborate stuffing could be a Nargissi *kofta ke baher* filling (page 55). Simply cover a hard-boiled quail egg with the mince mixture uncooked to the same size as the rice (about chicken egg size), and follow from stage 4 (without the rice, of course).

Serves: 4

BATARE MASALA
Curried Quail

When Arthur Hailey researched his novel Hotel he could have found his rags-to-riches hero in India, for the rise of one of India's grandest hotel chains has all the elements of fiction. Mohan Singh Oberoi arrived in Simla, the celebrated British hill station, in 1922, with a handful of small change and the clothes he stood up in. He got a job as a clerk at the best hotel in town, Clarkes. Only 12 years later, he had acquired enough assets to buy Clarkes. By 1938 he was able to buy a large hotel in Calcutta, which is now one of the world's best. Today the group has top properties in all India's major cities. The Calcutta Oberoi, the group's flagship, has 300 rooms and several restaurants, and India's best disco. It purifies the water supply ten times before it reaches the guests. Bombay's 700-room Oberoi Towers is the tallest building in India. Delhi's Oberoi Intercontinental is celebrated for its five restaurants, especially the Mughul Room which serves classy Indian food in spacious airy rooms decorated with plants and fountains. I had the following dish there, and afterwards I met the chef who gave me this recipe.

A former Delhi Oberoi chef is now in charge of cooking at **The Kensington Tandoori**, 1 Abingdon Road, London, W8. This dish is available there. This excellent restaurant has several other London restaurants in its group and one outside London, **The Last Viceroy**, Bourne End, Bucks.

4 whole quails (preferably boned)
2 tablespoons curry paste
3 oz (75 g) natural yoghurt

Gravy
2 tablespoons ghee
8 tablespoons curry masala gravy
1½ tablespoons gram flour (besan)
akhni stock or water
2 fl oz (50 ml) double cream
salt to taste

Spices
1 teaspoon turmeric
6 brown cardamoms
10 cloves
4 inch (10 cm) piece cassia bark
2 teaspoons white cummin seeds
1 teaspoon fennel seeds
½ teaspoon black cummin seeds
½–2 teaspoons chilli powder
½ teaspoon mango powder

Garnish
4 sheets silver leaf (*vark*)
2 tablespoons flaked almonds
1 tablespoon chopped fresh coriander leaves

1 Clean the quails then prick them all over. Mix the curry paste with the yoghurt in a large bowl, then cover the quails thoroughly. Leave to marinate in the fridge for a minimum of 6, a maximum of 30 hours.

2 To cook, preheat the oven to 325°F/160°C/Gas 3. Place the quails and their marinade on an oven tray and bake for 15 minutes.

3 Meanwhile, make the gravy. Heat the ghee in a karahi, and stir-fry the **Spices** for 1 minute. Add the curry masala gravy and heat until simmering.

4 Mix the flour with water to make a paste. Add it to the karahi, and as it thickens, add akhni stock or water to keep it from becoming too thick. Add the cream, and some salt to taste.

5 Take the quails from the oven – they should be cooked, with the marinade well caramelised. If not, finish under the grill. Place the quails in the karahi, and simmer for 5 minutes.

6 Garnish with silver leaf (page 157), and place the flaked almonds and chopped coriander on top of this.

Serves: 4

GAON ROAST DUCKLING

If you believed that marinated roast duckling was the sole preserve of the Pekinese Chinese, then I urge you to sample this recipe from **The Sonar Gaon**, *46 Upper Street, London, N1. Using the standard tandoori marinade the whole duckling is baked to produce a crispy, deep red, very tasty dish. (At the Sonar Gaon, the duckling would be cooked in the tandoor.) Optionally it could be stuffed with cooked rice or an apple, but I prefer to leave it unstuffed to allow the dripping (which can be used for future curry cooking) to escape easily into the drip tray.*

For four people use two 3½ lb (1.5 kg) ducks, and more marinade. Use the same timings.

**1 whole duckling, around
  3½ lb (1.5 kg)**

juice of 2 lemons

1 recipe tandoori marinade

1 Clean the duckling inside and out. Poke a sharp knife all over and deep into the duck then rub in the lemon juice and stand for half an hour in a deep bowl.

2 Strain and keep the spare lemon juice. Now work the tandoori marinade into the duck, and leave it to stand in the bowl for at least 6 hours.

3 Preheat the oven to 350°F/180°C/Gas 4. Whilst it is warming, remove the duck from the bowl, shaking off any excess marinade, and place on an oven tray. Smear some of the excess marinade back on to the duck, enough to give it an even coating. Place the duck into the oven. The total roasting time will be about 1¾ hours (allowing 30 minutes per lb/450 g).

4 After about 45 minutes, remove the duck and baste it with the remaining marinade. Return to the oven, and after 1½ hours pierce the plump part of the leg. When it is cooked the fluid that runs out will be clear; if not replace for longer. The marinade will have caramelised into a fantastic crispy coating. Place in a low oven to rest for 15 minutes, then cut into two servings, a half duck per person.

Serves: 2

SRI LANKAN DUCK

This highly aromatic curry recipe is based on one which I obtained from the Colombo Club, now incorporated into the new and luxurious **Taj Samudra Hotel***.*

Duck is enjoyed in Sri Lanka and suits this recipe very well. Ask for duck breasts. The best are **magret de canard***.*

4 duck breasts, about 8 oz (225 g) each

4 tablespoons fat rendered from the duck

2 tablespoons garlic purée

1 tablespoon ginger purée

8 tablespoons onion purée

$3\frac{1}{2}$ oz (90 g) creamed coconut

1 tablespoon brown sugar

7 fl oz (200 ml) tomato soup (about $\frac{1}{2}$ can)

1 tablespoon any vinegar

salt to taste

Spices (whole)

2 teaspoons coriander seeds

1 teaspoon cummin seeds

1 teaspoon fennel seeds

$\frac{1}{2}$ teaspoon fenugreek seeds

1 small piece cassia bark

$\frac{1}{2}$ teaspoon cloves

$\frac{1}{2}$ teaspoon green cardamoms

1 Preheat the oven to 375°F/190°C/Gas 5, and place the duck breasts on a rack on an oven tray. When the oven is hot, put the tray in, and roast for 25 minutes.

2 Meanwhile, in the same oven, place the **Spices** on another oven tray and roast for 3 minutes. Cool then grind to a fine dark powder. Make into a paste using a little water.

3 Remove the duck tray from the oven, and strain off the fat. Decide whether you want to use the skin. If yes, decide whether it needs more cooking to get it totally crispy. If it does, pull it away from the breast and return to the oven – if you don't want to use the skin, discard it.

4 Heat the rendered duck fat in a karahi and stir-fry the garlic, ginger and onion purées together for 4 minutes. Add the spice paste and stir-fry for a further 5 minutes.

5 Add the creamed coconut, sugar, tomato soup and vinegar. Stir-fry until simmering.

6 Cut the duck breasts into thin slices. Place them and the fried mixture into a casserole dish and return to the oven to finish off for about 20 more minutes. Add salt to taste.

Serves: 4

6
FISH

I fear that, like a great many English people, I am
very ignorant about fish. I quite enjoy fish when I
remember it exists, but my repertoire is, frankly,
limited to the old English favourites – cod, sole and
plaice. Yet a good fishmonger's slab is a work of art,
and a discussion with the experts is an education. I
visited a large multiple recently in a London suburb,
and this is what they had for sale, fresh, that day:
bream, haddock, hake, halibut, herring, John Dory,
lemon sole, mackerel, pike, plaice, salmon, sea bass,
sprats, trout, turbot and whiting. They also had the
following frozen fish: red snapper, red mullet,
sardines, shark steaks, swordfish steaks, tuna steaks
and whitebait.

And that was not all. Their shellfish department
was equally impressive, with fresh and frozen items
including Norwegian or Indian shelled frozen prawns,
200–300 to the pound (450 g), and Greenland shell-
on whole prawns, at 90–120 to the pound. King
prawns were 21–25, 16–20, 8–12 and around 5 to
the pound – the latter being freshwater 'shrimps'
from the River Ganges. They had various sizes of
Mediterranean crevettes, and jumbo scampi at 20–
30, 30–45 and 45–60 to the pound. There were also
clams, crab, crayfish (ecrevisse), crawfish (langouste),
lobster, monkfish, scallops (8–12 and 40–60 to the
pound), cockles, mussels, oysters, octopus, squid and
whelks.

I mention this, not because I have recipes for all of
these items, but to show the fantastic wealth of fish
and shellfish from which you can choose. You can
easily substitute one fish or shellfish for another.

GRILLED SPICED TROUT

The emperor Jahangir built his famous Kashmiri gardens in the 1600's. In their pools he kept large trout. In their noses he put gold rings. Their descendants still swim in those pools — sadly without their rings.

Fresh trout is delightful when cooked with spices, but it must *be fresh. The spicing itself can be very light indeed, as in this delicious recipe from* **Tithas** *restaurant, 31 High Street, Camberley, Surrey.*

**4 fresh trout, about 12 oz
    (350 g) each**

Spice marinade

1 teaspoon turmeric

1 teaspoon ground cummin

**1 teaspoon ground black
    pepper**

**4 tablespoons chopped
    fresh coriander leaves**

3 tablespoons mustard oil

1 teaspoon salt

1 Gut and carefully wash the trout clean, then dry them.

2 Mix the marinade ingredients together and coat the trout thoroughly, leaving it to absorb the flavours for about 1 hour.

3 When you are about to serve, grill or fry the fish — about 10 minutes — and serve at once. Tithas use their tandoor to cook the fish to achieve maximum flavour and, of course, they are perfect for the barbecue. Serve on a bed of lettuce with lemon wedges and onion rings.

Serves: *4 as a main course, 8 as a starter*

TANDOORI TROUT OR MACKEREL

This is another way to cook trout, using a tandoori marinade. You can use a proprietory tandoori paste for this, but it's better still to make your own (page 38). Here is the method used by the **Rajdoot**, *83 Park Street, Bristol, and its sister restaurants in Birmingham, Manchester and Dublin. Once again, serve for four as a main course, or eight as a starter.*

> **4 fresh trout, about 12 oz**
>   **(345 g) each (or mackerel**
>   **or salmon)**
> **1 recipe portion tandoori**
>   **marinade**

Proceed exactly as for grilled spiced trout, using the tandoori marinade. Serve similarly.

PATRANI MACHLI
Leaf (or Foil) Baked Fish

There is no other dish like this in the entire culinary repertoire of the sub-continent. Created by the Parsee community of Bombay, it is chunky fish (machli) coated with green herb paste and wrapped in a banana or patra leaf and steamed. Pomfret is the fish the Parsees use, but as it is not very easy to get hold of, it is quite acceptable to use alternatives such as cod or other fleshy white fish. Banana leaves are also hard to come by, so this method uses aluminium foil.

All this sounds complicated, but in fact the dish is really quite straight-forward. Nevertheless, only one restaurant in the UK attempts it – **The Bombay Brasserie**, *14 Courtfield Close, London SW7. Patrani machli is one of their most popular dishes.*

I like to serve this as a starter with no accompaniments, to get the most out of the fabulous flavours.

> **4 pieces filleted cod steak,**   **3 tablespoons mustard oil**
>   **about 8 oz (225 g) each**   **or vegetable oil**
>   **2 tablespoons any vinegar**

Coating

½ Spanish onion, peeled and
    coarsely chopped

2 bunches fresh coriander,
    leaves plus tender stalks

0–4 green chillies, coarsely
    chopped (to taste)

1 garlic clove

1 tablespoon coconut
    powder

1 teaspoon sugar

½ teaspoon salt

1 teaspoon ground cummin

juice of 1 lemon

Garnish

chopped fresh coriander

lemon wedges

1 Grind all the coating ingredients together in a blender or liquidiser.
    The paste should be of a thick porridge-like consistency. (If it is too
    thin put in a sieve to drain, and if too thick add a little water.)

2 Lay each piece of fish on a large piece of foil, then cover completely
    with paste, using up all the paste. Wrap the fish pieces lightly in
    the foil.

3 Meanwhile, put the oil and vinegar in an oven tray, and into an
    oven preheated to 375°F/190°C/Gas 5. When hot put the foiled
    fish into the tray and bake for 20 minutes.

5 To serve, carefully unwrap and discard the foil. The coating should
    have adhered to the fish and it should be quite moist. Pour all or
    some of the liquid in the pan over the dish. Garnish with fresh
    coriander and lemon wedges.

Serves: *4 as a starter*

MACHHER JHOL or MAACHLI JHAL
Bengali fish

The River Ganges is sacred to Hindus. Not only is it one of the world's largest rivers, it also contains a huge variety of freshwater fish, nowhere more prolific than at its tributaries and estuaries. Here the Ganges delta and its offshoot the Hougli divide Bengal from Bangladesh — but the cooking is much the same, and fish figures prominently.

Sadly though, although most of Britain's restaurants are Bangladeshi run, very few serve authentic fish dishes, saying that the British 'dislike' fish. I am certain that if more restaurants produced dishes like this one they would be bestsellers. I can only suggest you try this recipe from one of the country's best restaurants — the **Romna Gate Tandoori***, opposite Southgate tube station, London N14.*

$1\frac{1}{2}$ **lb (675 g) halibut or other firm white fish, filleted**

1 teaspoon turmeric

$\frac{1}{2}$ **teaspoon salt**

4 tablespoons mustard oil

1 teaspoon panch phoran

6 tablespoons curry masala gravy

6 fl oz (175 ml) akhni stock or water

Garnish

1 tablespoon chopped fresh coriander leaves or saffron strands

1 Mix the turmeric and salt into a runny paste with a tiny drop of water, and spread over the fish. Traditionally this is supposed both to enhance the flavour of the fish and reduce the odour during cooking.

2 Heat the oil in a large pan, then fry the panch phoran for 1 minute. Add the fish pieces, and fry each side for 2 minutes, turning once. Add the curry masala gravy, shake the pan to mix, and simmer for 2 minutes.

3 Add enough akhni stock or water to just cover the fish. Simmer for 10 minutes, always shaking the pan rather than stirring, which can break up the fish.

4 Remove the fish from the pan with a fish slice, and serve with a little of the gravy. Garnish with fresh coriander or saffron.

Serves: *4*

JINGHA HARA MASALA
Prawns in Green Herbs

I was staying at a delightful hotel south of Madras called **Fisherman's Cove***. On the first night I was there I watched the sun set over the sea, and as the last orange rays faded, about 20 tiny dhow-like boats with chugging engines appeared from a township about a mile down the beach. They had small sails and, as the sky went purple, little twinkling oil lights were lit on each boat. The fishing boats spread out and anchored about three miles out. They stayed immobile, twinkling all night. I got up early in the morning just as the sun was rising. When I got to the village the boats were being roped up and the entire population – women, children and old folk – were all pulling ropes, spreading sails and nets out on the sand to dry, and offering huge baskets to the fishermen to put the catch in. The contents of these baskets was amazing, with all sorts of sea creatures, but it was the shrimps that caught my eye – thousands of them, tiny and transparent. As I watched, two hotel chefs appeared and were handed a basket each. We walked back to the hotel together and they promised to cook some of those fresh shrimps for lunch. This is what they cooked.*

2 lb (900 g) brown shrimps, crevettes or prawns (200–300 to the lb/450 g)

3 tablespoons ghee or vegetable oil

salt

Paste

1 Spanish onion, peeled and coarsely chopped

2 tablespoons chopped fresh coriander leaves *or* coriander purée

1 tablespoon green masala paste

1 tablespoon chopped fresh mint leaves

2–6 fresh green chillies, coarsely chopped (to taste)

1 green capsicum pepper, seeded and coarsely chopped

2 tablespoons coconut powder or chunks of fresh coconut

1 For the paste, blend all the ingredients into a paste/purée.

2 Peel, wash or thaw the prawns.

3 In a frying pan or wok, heat the ghee or vegetable oil to medium. Add the prawns and fry for 2–3 minutes, then add the paste.

4 Simmer for about 10–15 minutes. Add a little green food colouring if you want a more vivid green colour.

Serves: 4

CHINGREE IN COCONUT
Coconut Shrimps

This recipe comes from Bangladesh, where the language is Bengali. Chingree means shrimp and is very similar to the Hindi word jinga *or* jingri. *Nowhere do shrimps or prawns grow bigger, more succulent or more tasty. Use medium size prawns (about 8–12 to the pound (450 g)) or larger and simply remove the head and the vein. This recipe is from owner/chef Tommy Miah, and is served at his* **Miah's Restaurant**, *Forrest Road, Edinburgh.*

2 lb (900 g) prawns

2 tablespoons vegetable oil

1 tablespoon black mustard
  seeds

1–4 teaspoons garlic purée

2 teaspoons ginger purée

1 medium onion, peeled and
  cut into rings

$2\frac{1}{2}$ oz (65 g) creamed
  coconut (about $\frac{1}{3}$ block)

1 tablespoon coconut
  powder

6 fl oz (175 ml) milk

juice of 1 lemon

0–3 fresh chillies, chopped
  (to taste)

salt to taste

Spices (roasted and ground)

2 teaspoons coriander

$\frac{1}{4}$ teaspoon fenugreek

1 teaspoon black
  peppercorns

6 curry leaves

1 De-head, de-vein, wash and dry the prawns.

2 Make a paste of the **Spices**, using a little water.

3 Heat the oil, fry the mustard seeds, the garlic and ginger then the spice paste, each for 1 minute, one after the other.

4 Add the onion rings and fry until translucent, then add the two coconuts and the milk. Stir-fry until the block dissolves, then add the lemon juice, chillies and salt.

5 When simmering, add the prawns. Stir-fry for 10 minutes, then serve.

Serves: 4

KING PRAWN MASALA

I've met a dish like this in various parts of India, including Bombay and Madras. This recipe from **Madhu's Brilliant Restaurant**, *39 South Road, Southall, Middlesex, uses prawns of small to medium size (about 16–20 to the pound), but you can use any size you wish. The dish, by the way, is one of the restaurant's most popular.*

2 lb (900 g) prawns	salt to taste
4 tablespoons ghee or vegetable oil	1 tablespoon chopped fresh coriander leaves
1 teaspoon garlic purée	1 tablespoon garam masala
1 teaspoon ginger purée	
8 tablespoons onion purée	*Spices*
0–4 green chillies (to taste)	$\frac{1}{2}$ teaspoon turmeric
6 medium tomatoes	$\frac{1}{2}$ teaspoon chilli powder

1 De-shell and de-vein the prawns.

2 Whilst heating the oil, mix together the garlic, ginger and onion purées in a blender with the chilli, and blend again.

3 Stir-fry this purée in the hot oil for 5 minutes until golden, then add the **Spices**. Fry for 2 more minutes.

4 Meanwhile, purée the tomatoes, then add them to your pan. Stir-fry until the mixture reduces a little – about 10 minutes – and becomes a darker red.

5 Add the prawns and simmer for about 10 minutes, before salting to taste.

6 Toss in the chopped coriander and garam masala. Stir-fry for 3–5 minutes, then serve.

Serves: 4

JEERA PRAWN
Prawns Stir-Fried in Cummin Seeds

A little spice can go a long way, for all that is used to make this an astonishingly tasty dish is cummin seeds and turmeric. But here's a tip. Prawns can be a bit tasteless, especially frozen ones which, when thawed, turn out to have contained more water than meat. A very tasty prawn is the Norwegian hand-peeled prawn, which comes 150–200 to the pound (450 g), packed in 1 kg tubs in brine. They are expensive but they keep in the fridge in their brine, and the extra flavour is certainly worth the expense. Jeera prawn makes an excellent starter (halve the quantities given here) or main course, and takes less than 15 minutes to prepare and cook.

Jeera prawn is to be found at some of the better restaurants, such as **The Viceroy of India***, 50 St Helen's Road, Swansea.*

$1\frac{1}{2}$ lb (675 g) prawns in brine, or thawed frozen or fresh

6 tablespoons mustard oil

2 tablespoons whole white cummin seeds

2 pink onions, *or* 1 Spanish onion, peeled and finely chopped

2 teaspoons garlic purée

2 teaspoons ginger purée

$1\frac{1}{2}$ teaspoons turmeric

1 red capsicum pepper, cut into julienne strips

1–4 green chillies, finely chopped (to taste)

salt and pepper

1 Prepare the prawns, draining, drying etc as appropriate.

2 Heat the oil to hot in a karahi, and fry the cummin seeds for 30 seconds – until they 'pop'. Then add the onion and fry until it starts to crisp. Add the garlic, ginger and turmeric, stir-fry for 2 minutes then add the capsicum pepper and chilli. Add a very little water or some of the brine to prevent sticking.

3 After 2 more minutes, add the prawns and simmer for enough time to get them good and hot, about 5 minutes (no longer or prawns go rubbery). Serve at once.

Serves: 4

LOBSTER KORMA

A century after the Portuguese, the English discovered India and in 1608 obtained the permission of the Moghuls to trade. They set up their first docks at Surat (north of Bombay), but they had it in mind to establish trading stations around India, in areas outside direct Moghul control. They chose three virgin sites with good potential anchorages. Factories came first, then townships and finally armies to defend them. Madras was established in 1640, Bombay in 1674 and Calcutta in 1690. Calcutta was the British capital of India until 1911, and with its abundance of seaboard and river estuaries, the area has always been notable for fish and seafood. Massive lobsters there are almost ten-a-penny. This lobster korma from the **Indus Curry Tandoori,** *70a High Street, Colchester, is especially tasty.*

4 lobsters or crawfish,
   about 1 lb (450 g) each
3 tablespoons ghee
6 tablespoons onion purée
6–8 fl oz (175–250 ml)
   akhni stock
1 teaspoon saffron
1 tablespoon chopped fresh
   coriander leaves
salt to taste

Marinade

3 oz (75 g) natural yoghurt
1 tablespoon garlic purée
1 tablespoon ginger purée

Spices

2 inch (5 cm) piece cassia
   bark
6 green cardamoms

1 Boil the lobsters, if fresh, for 15 minutes. If frozen, thaw. When cool, cleave the shells in two and pick out all the flesh. Chop it into bite-sized pieces. (Discard the shells or use them to serve the korma in.)

2 Mix the marinade ingredients in a large bowl. Place the lobster pieces in the marinade and leave for 1 hour.

3 After an hour, heat the ghee and stir-fry the onion purée for 5 minutes. Add the spices and the akhni stock, and heat to simmering.

4 Add the lobster, and cook for 10 minutes. Add the saffron, fresh coriander and salt to taste. Mix and serve.

Serves: 4

7

VEGETABLES

Southern India has been mostly vegetarian since the Dravidian tribes occupied it many thousands of years ago. Vegetarianism in the north of India came much later with the establishment of the Hindu religion in around 1000 BC with the veneration of the cow. Of today's Indian population of some 700 million, probably in excess of 75 per cent are vegetarian.

Nowhere on earth are vegetables cooked more effectively than in India. Spicing and curry-making techniques elevate humble ingredients to great dishes. Take lentils, for example. By the addition of a few spices, ordinary red lentils are as tasty as any curry, and served with rice or bread make a very economical and nutritious complete meal.

I have selected a varied range of recipes which incorporate many different vegetables and techniques. Bear in mind also that many of the recipes in the previous chapters can be adapted to your choice of vegetable.

A trip to an Asian community greengrocer is an amazing experience. There you will see tray upon tray of unfamiliar vegetables of all types. These and many others are everyday items to the Indian cook, but most of us do not have access to such produce. In any case, much of it is very bitter or unpalatable to the Western palate, so I have excluded the real oddities from my recipes.

Many of the dishes following can be served as a vegetarian main course. If required as a vegetable accompaniment only, simply halve the ingredients.

VEGETABLE BHAJEE

*This is the standard vegetable curry — bhajee meaning cooked vegetables — and it appears on the menu of most curry houses. It has no specific regional origin in the sub-continent so there are many variations of the dish, but in general terms it is any combination of vegetables in a curry sauce — potatoes, cauliflower, carrot and peas being most commonly encountered at the restaurant where, incidentally, this dish is very popular. It can be easily spoiled by overcooking the vegetables — and as vegetables take different lengths of time to boil, it is important to pre-cook them individually first. This is the way they do it at one of Edinburgh's best restaurants — **The Verandah**, 17 Dalry Road, Edinburgh.*

As a main course

$1\frac{1}{2}$ lb (675 g) vegetables made up as follows: potatoes, peeled and cubed, carrots, sliced, frozen peas and frozen beans

2 tablespoons sunflower oil

1 tablespoon curry masala paste

12 tablespoons onion purée

1 tablespoon chopped fresh coriander leaves

salt to taste

akhni stock or water

1 Boil the vegetables to near readiness — crisp but not mushy. If the vegetables are to be used later, rinse them in cold water and strain.

2 Heat the oil and stir-fry the curry masala paste for 1 minute then the onion purée for 5 minutes. Add in the vegetables when simmering, followed by the fresh coriander and salt to taste. Add water or stock to get as runny a consistency as you want.

3 Serve promptly.

Serves: 4

VIGAN BHAJEE

*This is a variation on the previous recipe from **The Magna**, 50 Tavistock Street, Bedford. Vigan (or Vegan) describes people who are true vegetarians. This means they eat no dairy products at all, including butter, ghee, yoghurt and eggs. You can use any vegetables of your choice for this dish, but the following is a tasty combination.*

1½ lb (675 g) vegetables, made up as follows: parsnip, peeled and cubed, sweet potatoes, peeled and cubed, courgettes, sliced and frozen petits pois.

2 tablespoons sunflower oil

1 teaspoon turmeric

1 teaspoon garlic purée

12 tablespoons onion purée

1 tablespoon curry masala paste

1 tablespoon chopped fresh coriander leaves

salt to taste

akhni stock or water

Cook everything as in the previous recipe, stir-frying the turmeric for 20 seconds then the garlic for 1 minute, the onion for 3 minutes and the paste for 1 minute.

Serves: 4 as a main course

BINDI BHAJEE
Okra Curry

Bindis are okra or 'ladies' fingers'. They are rather pithy, ribbed, green, chilli-shaped, pointed vegetables with a stalk varying in size from around 2 inches (5 cm) to 4 inches (10 cm) and more.

*Bindis are rather difficult to cook. The first factor is careful selection. It is usually better to choose smaller ones – the large ones are often scaly. To prepare them, wash them carefully. Dry them, then cut off the point and trim off the stalk. Do not cook them in water, otherwise they ooze sap while cooking. Even slight overcooking results in a soggy mush and again that sticky sap. It's most unpleasant, and unfortunately this is one of those dishes which many standard curry houses get wrong. It can only be successful if it is cooked fresh. A microwave is the best of all, giving lovely crisp results. One restaurant which always gets this dish right is the **Chesham Tandoori**, 48 Broad Street, Chesham, Bucks.*

In Bengali, this dish is called dherosh chach-chori, *and in the south of India* vendaika.

$1\frac{1}{2}$ lb (675 g) okra

6 tablespoons mustard oil

2 teaspoons mustard seeds

4 tablespoons chopped onion (preferably small pink ones for flavour and colour)

juice of 1 lemon

1 tablespoon brown sugar

2 tomatoes, finely chopped

1 tablespoon chopped fresh coriander leaves

salt to taste

Spices 1 (ground)

$\frac{1}{2}$ teaspoon turmeric

1 teaspoon cummin

1 teaspoon coriander

$\frac{1}{2}$ teaspoon chilli powder

1 teaspoon garlic powder

Spices 2

1 teaspoon ground cassia bark

$\frac{1}{2}$ teaspoon green cardamom seeds (not pods)

1 Carefully wash the okra then dry them. Cut off the pointed tip and the stalk and discard.

2 Mix **Spices 1** into a paste with a little water.

3 Heat the oil in a karahi. Stir-fry the mustard seeds until they pop, about 1 minute then add the spice paste and fry for 2 minutes, then the onion for 3 minutes.

4 Meanwhile, chop the okra into 1 inch (2.5 cm) pieces, add them to the karahi straightaway, and gently toss for 5 minutes.

5 Add the lemon juice, sugar, tomato, **Spices 2** and fresh coriander.

6 Stir-fry carefully for 5 more minutes. If the okra were tender to start with they are now cooked perfectly. Add salt to taste.

7 Serve at once. Do not store or freeze this dish – it will go sappy and mushy.

Serves: 4 as a main course

MUSHROOM BHAJEE

*One of my favourite dishes, but only if the mushrooms are absolutely fresh —
white button ones are best. Do not stew them — in fact simply add them whole
or quartered, or thinly sliced in a food processor, coat them with the hot gravy
and serve at once. This dish does not keep or freeze. Here is a method from
the* **Asha Restaurant***, 79 Bold Street, Liverpool, Merseyside.*

$1\frac{1}{2}$ lb (675 g) mushrooms

3 tablespoons vegetable oil
  (sesame or sunflower)

2 teaspoons garlic purée

6 tablespoons onion purée

akhni stock or water

0–2 fresh chillies, chopped
  (to taste)

1 tablespoon chopped fresh
  coriander leaves

salt to taste

Spices (ground)

1 teaspoon coriander

1 teaspoon cummin

2 teaspoons paprika

$\frac{1}{2}$ teaspoon turmeric

1 Wash the mushrooms, and only peel them if they look as though
   they need it. Leave whole, or quarter or thinly slice them.

2 Heat the oil and fry the garlic at quite high heat for just 1 minute.
   Add the onion and fry for about 3–5 minutes. They should be
   golden brown.

3 Make a paste of the **Spices** with a little vegetable stock or water,
   and add to the onion. Fry for a further 5 minutes then add sufficient
   water or stock to obtain a thick but fluid mixture. When it is
   simmering, add the mushrooms and the fresh chilli and coriander.
   When they are hot they are ready to serve — and the fresher the
   better. Add salt to taste.

Serves: 4 as an accompaniment

Right
On the Thali tray: (anti-clockwise) *Quick Lemon Rice* **(page 150),** *Jardaloo Sali Boti* **(pages
70–1),** *Sali* **(page 73),** *Cachumber Punjabi* **(page 168),** *Coconut Chutney* **(page 168),** *Paneer*
(page 41), Centre: *Puri* **(page 163), In the Karahi:** *Bundghobi Poriyal* **(page 136), Below:**
Lobster Korma **(page 123),** *Plain Boiled Rice* **(pages 148–9).**

SAG WALA
Spinach Curry

Sag *means spinach and* wala *means cooked (it also means a tradesman, and the* punka wala, *for example, was the servant who operated the ceiling fan in the old days). This dish is more commonly called sag bhajee, but we use the name that the* **Jhorna**, *32c High Street, Orpington, Kent uses for their recipe for the dish.*

1½ lb (675 g) fresh or frozen
   spinach

6 tablespoons vegetable
   ghee

2 6 garlic cloves, thinly
   sliced

½ Spanish onion, peeled and
   finely chopped

0–4 fresh green chillies,
   chopped (to taste)

4 tablespoons curry gravy

salt to taste

Spices

½ teaspoon black cummin
   seeds

1 teaspoon white cummin
   seeds

1 Wash the grit out of the spinach leaves if using fresh, or thaw if using frozen leaf. Chop it up. Blanch fresh leaves in boiling water for 3–4 minutes. Strain.

2 Heat the ghee and stir-fry the garlic for 1 minute, then the **Spices** for 1 minute. Add the onion and fresh chilli and stir-fry for a further 3 minutes.

3 Add the gravy, and when simmering add the spinach and salt to taste. Briskly stir around until hot. Serve or keep warm. It will freeze, but it is safe to do so only with fresh spinach.

Serves: 4 as a main dish

Left
Some Vegetable Delights: *Niramish* **(page 132),** *Sag Wala* **(page 129),** *Chana Chat* **(page 52),** *Bombay Potato* **(page 141).**

NAVRATTAN KORMA
Nine Mildly Curried Vegetables

Nine vegetables (excluding garlic, ginger, onion and coriander) is a lot so you may wish to make this dish for special occasions. It is a good party dish, particularly if you choose and cut your vegetables in a way that obtains interesting contrasts of colour and shapes.

The number nine is very significant. Akbar was perhaps the greatest Moghul emperor, and during his reign in the sixteenth century he gave the most talented men in the empire special places at court. They were nine. Included in this elite 'club' were not only Akbar's heads of state and his generals, there was his most fabled musician, poet and philosopher. The nine met frequently with the Emperor to fulfil Akbar's great ideals. They became known as the Navratna — the nine jewels of the empire. Even Akbar's chefs were inspired — the recipe for this dish was created then and has come down doubtless unaltered in the time-honoured way — by word of mouth.

I met this dish for the first time in Agra (Akbar's capital city) at the restaurant named in honour of the nine, The Navrattan, at the Mugal Sheraton Hotel. Virtually the same dish is on the menu of the elegant **Viceroy of India** *restaurant, 2 Glentworth Street, London NW1.*

Use nine vegetables of your choice, and the nett weight after preparing should be $1\frac{1}{2}$ lb (675 g). Choose vegetables which give good contrasting colours and which can be given approximately the same shape when cut. The following is my selection of nine.

$1\frac{1}{2}$ lb (675 g) vegetables: carrot, potato, swede, parsnip, mooli (white radish), peas, runner beans, yellow and red capsicum pepper

3 tablespoons vegetable oil

20 almonds

1 teaspoon garlic purée

1 teaspoon ginger purée

8 tablespoons onion purée

0–4 fresh green chillies, chopped (to taste, optional)

1 tablespoon chopped fresh coriander leaves

10 fl oz ($\frac{1}{2}$ pint) milk

akhni stock or water

1 tablespoon sultanas (optional)

2 teaspoons garam masala

1 teaspoon saffron

7 fl oz (200 ml) single cream

1 teaspoon sugar (optional)

salt to taste

Spices

$\frac{1}{2}$ teaspoon fennel seeds

$\frac{1}{2}$ teaspoon black cummin seeds

1 teaspoon green cardamoms

2 inch (5 cm) piece cassia bark

1 Prepare the vegetables. Blanch the first five, then dice them into $\frac{1}{2}$ inch (1.25 cm) cubes. Slice the beans to the same length, and the peppers into diamond shapes.

2 Heat the oil in a karahi and fry the almonds for 2 minutes. Drain the almonds well and set aside. Using the same oil, stir-fry the **Spices** for 1 minute, then the garlic for 1 minute, the ginger for 1 minute, and the onion for 5 minutes. Add the chilli if using and fresh coriander.

3 Add all the vegetables and the milk, and simmer for 5 minutes. Add stock or water if you want a runnier consistency.

4 Add the sultanas, fried almonds, garam masala, saffron, cream, sugar and salt to taste. When simmering it is ready to serve. It should be nice and creamy and very colourful, and it goes well with a dry dish such as stuffed quails, accompanied by naan or stuffed aubergines and rice.

Serves: 4

NIRAMISH
Stir-Fried Mixed Vegetables

A Bengali recipe devised, it is said, for newly widowed Hindu women, niramish is also called shukto niramis Turkari. The recipe contains no onion and very little spicing, which it is supposed will keep the widows' sexual appetites down! Cooked in mustard oil with panch phoran and lemon juice, the mix of lightly cooked vegetables gives a nutty taste.

Use your own choice of fresh vegetables in season. Simply blanch them then stir-fry with subtle spices and herbs to produce a crispy crunchy side or main dish, full of vitamins and health giving nutrients as well as taste. This recipe is given by the **Polash**, *86 West Street, Shoeburyness, Essex.*

$1\frac{1}{2}$ lb (675 g) vegetables:
  any four of okra, Kenyan
  beans, cauliflower,
  marrow, carrot, potato,
  peas
6 tablespoons mustard oil
juice of 1 lemon
1 tablespoon chopped fresh
  coriander leaves
salt to taste

Spices
2 teaspoons panch phoran
$\frac{1}{2}$ teaspoon turmeric
$\frac{1}{2}$–2 teaspoons chilli powder

1 Prepare the vegetables, and blanch those which need it. If using okra, prepare as on pages 126–7.

2 Heat the oil, and fry the **Spices** for 1 minute. Stir-fry the okra first, if being used, for 2 minutes. Then add the other vegetables. Stir-fry for 7–8 more minutes.

3 Then add the lemon juice, fresh coriander and salt to taste. Toss for 2–3 more minutes. Serve fresh. Will keep or freeze but this is not ideal – the crispness goes.

Serves: *4 as a main course*

SABZI DILRUBA
Vegetables in a Creamy Sauce

This is a choice of vegetables cooked with crumbled paneer, *eggs and nuts in a creamy sauce. The dish can trace its roots directly to Iran (where* sabzi *also means vegetables), containing a typical Persian combination of tastes and textures. The dish is one of the specialities of* **The Kalpna**, *2 St Patrick Square, Edinburgh, a vegetarian restaurant.*

$1\frac{1}{2}$ lb (675 g) vegetables,
   made up as follows:
   1 large marrow (about
     1 lb/450 g)
   4 oz (115 g) each of peas
     and runner beans
2 tablespoons vegetable oil
8 tablespoons curry gravy
2 tomatoes, quartered
1 recipe paneer, crumbled
3 tablespoons peanuts
6–8 whole quails' eggs,
   hard-boiled for 4
   minutes, *or* 2 hens' eggs,
   hard-boiled and chopped
2 fl oz (50 ml) single cream

Spices
$\frac{1}{2}$ teaspoon turmeric
1 teaspoon ground cummin
1 teaspoon ground
   coriander
$\frac{1}{4}$ teaspoon fenugreek seeds
$\frac{1}{4}$ teaspoon asafoetida

1 Peel the marrow and cut into cubes. To blanch it, place in a strainer over a pan of boiling water, with the lid on the strainer, so the marrow is not immersed, then steam for 10 minutes.

2 Heat the oil. Stir-fry the **Spices** for 1 minute, then add the curry gravy and fry for a further 5 minutes.

3 Add the tomato, peas and beans and simmer for 3 minutes. Add the crumbled paneer, peanuts, whole or chopped eggs, marrow and cream. Add a little water if you require it, and some salt to taste. Serve when simmering.

Serves: *4 as a main course*

KAYLA FOOGATH
Banana Curry

A foogath is a particular method of vegetable cooking in the south of India. It will be found in the Malabar area so it is more than apt that this dish is found on the unusual menu of the **Malabar** *restaurant, Uxbridge Street, London W8. The principal vegetable in this case is* kayla *or* banana, *and providing you don't overcook it it is superb. But you can* foogath *any vegetable or combination. Note the near absence of spicing in the Malabar's recipe.*

4 dessert bananas, peeled and chopped	$\frac{1}{2}$ green capsicum pepper, seeded and sliced
2 tablespoons ghee or mustard oil (or walnut oil)	1 tomato, chopped
	salt to taste
juice of 1 lemon	chilli powder to taste

1 Heat the oil and add the bananas, followed by the other ingredients.
2 Heat up to the sizzling stage, gently toss, and serve immediately.

Serves: *4 generously as an accompaniment*

AVIAL
Malabar Mixed Vegetables

Avial is known as the Malabar masterpiece. It is traditionally made from a combination of yoghurt and vegetables and does not use tamarind and dhal (they are less available there). Traditionally the dish would contain a combination of some of the following, aubergine, plantain, yam, drumstick, pumpkin, snake, bitter and ash gourd. Also used are potato, stalks of spinach or broccoli, cucumber and carrot. Mandatory is green (sour) mango, yoghurt and coconut.

Avial is prepared on certain occasions at the great temples of the south for mass feedings in vast brass urns, 5 feet (1.5 metres) high and 10 feet (3 metres) in diameter, and is a tradition which goes back to the Chola temple builders of the tenth century.

One of the most exciting trends in the Indian restaurant scene of the last few years has been the arrival of vegetarian restaurants serving South Indian food. As with any vegetarian cooking, the food must be brought to the table *piping hot, freshly cooked — no reheating of yesterday's food — and crisp, not mushy. Nowhere is vegetarian food more interesting than South India, and nowhere is it cooked better than at **Sabras**, 263 High Road, London NW10. Avial is one of their speciality dishes.*

$1\frac{1}{2}$ lb (675 g) mixed vegetables

the flesh of $\frac{1}{2}$ a fresh coconut and its water, or 2 tablespoons coconut powder or desiccated coconut, mixed to a paste with water

2–4 fresh green chillies, roughly chopped (to taste)

2 teaspoons cummin seeds

1 teaspoon turmeric

1 small sour mango, skinned, stoned and chopped (or 1 teaspoon mango powder)

2 oz (50 g) natural yoghurt

10 curry leaves

salt to taste

4 tablespoons coconut oil

coconut powder if required

1 Prepare and trim the vegetables, as appropriate. The tradition is to cut them into thinnish diamond-shaped slices.

2 Make a paste in a blender/processor of the coconut, chillies, cummin seeds and turmeric with the coconut water. Add a little water if necessary.

3 Blanch the vegetables for 3–4 minutes in plenty of water then strain, leaving enough blanching water to cover the vegetables.

4 Add the mango flesh, yoghurt curry leaves and the paste. Simmer for a short while until the vegetables are ready. Add salt to taste.

5 Just prior to serving, heat and add the coconut oil. If it is very watery (controllable at stage 3), add some coconut powder to thicken it.

Serves: *4 as a main course*

BUNDGHOBI PORIYAL
South Indian Shredded Cabbage

Since time immemorial the Dhaka area in Bangladesh has been famed for its exquisite textiles, called jamundi *and locally known as* mul-mul *and as muslin in the West. The fabric was so fine that a dress made of it could pass through a wedding ring. The industry flourished under the Moghuls, and the tradition continued in Britain in the last century when Queen Victoria's wedding dress was made from muslin.*

The fabric is used as decoration in the **Jamandi** *restaurant in central London run by the man who achieves more publicity than any other restaurateur in his field, Amin Ali. He also runs The Red Fort, 77 Dean Street, London W1. The Jamandi, 34 Charlotte Street, London W1 serves high-quality Indian regional food and this is one of their speciality dishes.*

1 white cabbage, about 1$\frac{1}{2}$ lb (675 g) in weight, shredded in a food processor	1 large Spanish onion, peeled and finely chopped
4 tablespoons coconut oil or mustard oil	1 tablespoon chopped fresh coriander leaves
1 teaspoon mustard seeds	flesh of 1 coconut, shredded, and its water
	salt to taste

1   Blanch the shredded cabbage in boiling water for 1–2 minutes, then strain.

2   Heat the oil and fry the mustard seeds for 2 minutes, the onion for 3 minutes, then the fresh coriander for 1 minute.

3   Place the cabbage in the pan and stir-fry until hot. Use coconut water to keep it moist. Add the shredded coconut. Salt to taste and serve. Garnish, if you like, as the Jamundi does, with some steamed white lentils (urid dhal) and fresh coriander.

Serves: *4 as an accompaniment*

STUFFED PEPPER CURRY
Bhare Mirchi

Whole green peppers stuffed with spicy mashed potatoes and braised in a curry sauce, this makes a delicious vegetarian main course, served with Indian bread.

There are many vegetables which offer themselves as candidates for stuffing including potatoes, capsicum peppers, tomatoes, mushrooms (fiddly but nice), marrows and aubergines (see next recipe). I've even come across apples and mangoes scooped out and stuffed with curry. Use your imagination!

I have not come across this particular dish in many restaurants and I'm not sure why not — it is not difficult to make, yet it looks excellent. One restaurant which does prepare 'home-made-style' Indian food is **Nirmal's**, *193 Glossop Road, Sheffield, South Yorkshire. Mrs Nirmal herself does the cooking and the day's specials are chalked up on a blackboard.*

4 medium to large firm
   green or red capsicum
   peppers

Potato filling
2 large potatoes, about
   12 oz (350 g) in total,
   peeled
1 medium onion, peeled and
   chopped
2 fresh green chillies,
   chopped
½ teaspoon garam masala
salt

Sauce
1 medium onion, peeled and
   finely chopped
2 garlic cloves, finely chopped
1 inch (2.5 cm) piece fresh ginger
vegetable oil
10 fl oz (300 ml) stock or
   tomato juice
salt

Sauce spices
1 teaspoon each of turmeric,
cummin seeds, garam masala

1   For the potato filling, boil the potatoes, then mash them.
2   Add the onion, chillies and garam masala, with salt to taste.
3   For the sauce, fry the onion, garlic and ginger in some oil until golden (about 15 minutes).
4   Make a paste of the **Sauce spices** with a little water, then add to the fried mixture.
5   Fry for 5–10 minutes, stirring frequently, then add stock or tomato juice and some salt. Simmer until needed (stage 9).
6   To prepare the peppers, cut the stalk end off, leaving a hole of 2 inches (5 cm) diameter. Carefully remove the pithy centre and seeds.
7   Blanch for 2 minutes in boiling water.
8   Fill each pepper with the cooked potato filling, and place in an oven dish which enables the peppers to stand upright without falling over.
9   Gently pour the sauce into the oven dish and cook for 15–20 minutes in an oven preheated to 325°F/160°C/Gas 3.

Serves: *4 as a main course*

STUFFED BABY AUBERGINE

The art of all vegetable cooking is to produce a dish which is not overcooked or mushy, but timed to crispy perfection. It is much harder to do this with vegetables than with meat, particularly in the busy restaurant kitchen — the margins of error are smaller.

One restaurant which reflects state-of-the-art vegetarian cookery is the **Munbhave**, *305 London Road, Croydon. This tiny establishment is run by a Gujerati husband and wife team, and the cooking is indistinguishable from that of the Indian home. This dish is one of their most popular specialities.*

**8 small aubergines, about
  2–3 oz (50–75 g) each**

Stuffing

2 tablespoons vegetable oil

**$\frac{1}{4}$ Spanish onion, peeled and
  finely chopped**

**1–4 green chillies, finely
  chopped (to taste)**

4 tablespoons frozen peas

**1 tablespoon chopped fresh
  coriander leaves**

**1 tablespoon freshly grated
  coconut (or desiccated)**

**1 tablespoon raw cashew
  nuts, chopped**

**1 tablespoon raisins,
  chopped (optional)**

salt to taste

Spices

**1 teaspoon ground
  coriander**

**1 teaspoon cummin seeds,
  roasted**

1 teaspoon garam masala

$\frac{1}{4}$ teaspoon asafoetida

1 Make the stuffing first, allowing it to cool, at least enough to handle. Heat the oil and stir-fry the onion for 2 minutes. Add the **Spices** and stir-fry for a further 2 minutes.

2 Add all the remaining stuffing ingredients, mix well and cook for another 2 minutes, creating a dry mixture. Remove from heat and leave to cool. (This quantity is generous — if you have spare stuffing, freeze for future use in any curry base.)

3 When ready for the final stage, boil some water. Wash the aubergines, and blanch them for 3 minutes.

4 Cut off the stalk and slit each aubergine to create a pocket. Carefully stuff the pocket with the filling. Place the filled aubergines in an oven tray and into the oven — preheated to 325°F/160°C/Gas 3 —

for about 15 minutes. Serve straightaway – the dish does not keep or freeze, it goes mushy. If you want to serve a gravy with it, a delicious Gujarati gravy is *kudhi* (page 45).

Serves: 4 as an accompaniment

PANEER KORMA

In this recipe, paneer is compressed and cut into cubes then deep-fried. The cubes have very little taste, but combined in a creamy sauce this recipe from **The Mandeer** *restaurant, 21 Hanway Place, London W1 makes a delicious curry. The recipe for home-made paneer is on page 41.*

1 recipe home-made paneer

4 tablespoons butter ghee

1 inch (2.5 cm) cube fresh ginger, cut into julienne

1 Spanish onion, peeled and thinly sliced

about 3 oz (75 g) natural yoghurt

2 tablespoons gram flour (besan)

2 teaspoons brown sugar

2 teaspoons tomato purée

1 pint (600 ml) paneer whey

20 strands saffron

1 tablespoon chopped fresh coriander leaves

Spices 1 (ground)

1 teaspoon cummin

1 teaspoon turmeric

1 teaspoon coriander

1 teaspoon garlic powder

Spices 2 (whole)

12 green cardamoms

4 cloves

1 teaspoon white cummin seeds

$\frac{1}{2}$ teaspoon black cummin seeds

$\frac{1}{2}$ teaspoon fennel seeds or aniseed

2 star anises

1 Make a paste of **Spices 1** with a little water.
2 Heat the ghee and stir-fry **Spices 2** for 1 minute, the ginger for 2 minutes, and the onion for 5 minutes. Now add the spice paste, and stir-fry for 3 more minutes.
3 Add the yoghurt and the gram flour, sugar and tomato purée. Stir in well, then add the whey.
4 Salt to taste and add the paneer. When simmering, add the saffron and coriander. Serve after 2 more minutes.

Serves: 4 as an accompaniment

MALAI KOFTA
Vegetable Balls in Cream Sauce

Kofta means round or ball shaped. This kofta uses mashed potato as the main ingredient of the balls, which are deep-fried then, just prior to serving, simmered in a curry sauce containing cream (malai). Marrow or other gourds are most commonly used for this dish and are extremely popular in India (grate and bind with mashed potato and gram flour), but you could use any vegetable which shreds easily. Koftas need to be freshly made, thus they are rarely found on restaurant menus. **The Palace Tandoori**, *106 Fulham Palace Road, London W6 is one establishment where they can be tasted.*

Koftas

1 lb (450 g) mashed potato

1 tablespoon raisins

2 tablespoons cashew nuts, ground

1 tablespoon curry powder

$\frac{1}{2}$ teaspoon salt

1 teaspoon sugar

Sauce

4 tablespoons mustard oil

1 tablespoon curry masala paste

2 teaspoons garlic purée

2 teaspoons ginger purée

8 tablespoons onion purée

5 fl oz (150 ml) akhni stock or water

1 teaspoon tomato purée

6 tablespoons vegetable oil

4 oz (100 g) paneer, cut into $\frac{1}{4}$ in (6 mm) cubes

12 whole cashew nuts

Garnish

1 tablespoon double cream

1 To make the koftas, mix together all the ingredients. The mixture should be glutinous enough to form into 'dumpling' balls. Set aside.

2 For the sauce, heat the mustard oil in a pan and stir-fry the curry paste for 1 minute, then the garlic for 1 minute, the ginger for 1 minute, and the onion for 5 minutes. Add the stock or water and tomato purée and simmer.

3 Heat the vegetable oil in a karahi, and stir-fry the paneer and nuts together until both are golden (it only takes a couple of minutes so it is worth concentrating). Strain well, and put the paneer and nuts into the sauce. Keep warm.

4 Heat the same oil in the karahi, and very carefully fry the koftas until they are hot throughout, and golden in colour (about 4–5 minutes).

5 To serve, place the balls in a serving dish. Put the warm sauce over them and garnish with the cream.

Serves: 4 *as a main course*

BOMBAY POTATO

I am quite certain about one thing . . . if you stood on a street corner in Bombay and asked passers-by to describe Bombay potato they would give you blank looks. I've never come across this dish either in Bombay or the whole of India. Yet every standard curry house has the dish on its menu and it is one of their most popular dishes, albeit as an accompanying dish. Potatoes — especially new ones — are excellent curry subjects. This is a simple dish: potatoes boiled then simmered in a curry sauce and we asked the **Mumtaz**, 36 *Cowgate, Peterborough, Cambs, for their recipe.*

$1\frac{1}{2}$ lb (675 g) new potatoes (or large, older ones, quartered), cooked

4 tablespoons vegetable oil

8 tablespoons curry gravy

2 tomatoes, roughly chopped

salt to taste

Spices

2 teaspoons garam masala

1 teaspoon turmeric

$\frac{1}{2}$–2 teaspoons chilli powder

$\frac{1}{2}$ teaspoon mango powder

1 Heat the oil, and stir-fry the **Spices** for 30 seconds, then add the curry gravy. Stir-fry for 2 minutes then add the tomatoes and simmer for 5 more minutes.

2 Now add the cooked potato, and simmer until hot. Salt to taste.

Serves: 4 *as an accompaniment*

ALOO PODIMAS
South Indian Potato

On long journeys on Indian Railways, your food is ordered and paid for at a stop en-route, then delivered to your carriage piping-hot at the next stop for you to eat as the train pulls on. The dirty dishes are collected at the next (third) stop. This potato dish was one that I had in this way on a train journey in Southern India. The system seems to be very complex, but it works right down to the last detail – the waiter even had the meal in his hands and was standing on the platform in exactly the right place to enter my carriage when the train stopped.

$1\frac{1}{2}$ lb (675 g) potato, peeled
   and diced

2 teaspoons turmeric

6 tablespoons mustard oil

1 tablespoon urid dhal,
   crushed

1 Spanish onion, peeled and
   thinly sliced

3 tomatoes, chopped

salt to taste

Spices

2 teaspoons mustard seeds

8 dry curry leaves

1–6 dry red chillies (to
   taste)

1 teaspoon paprika

1 Boil the potato dice with the turmeric until still a little 'crisp'.

2 Meanwhile, heat the oil in a karahi and fry the **Spices** and the dhal for 2 minutes.

3 Add the onion slices and fry until brown (around 5 minutes).

4 Add the tomatoes to the pan and simmer until cooked (about 5 minutes).

5 Add the just-cooked potatoes, and toss well. Add salt to taste, then serve. This dish will keep chilled for a day. Freezing spoils the texture of the potato.

Serves: *4 as a main course*

ALOO MAKHANWALLA
Potato in Tandoori Sauce

One airline succeeds in providing the best airborne meals you will find anywhere. Air India flies to 36 cities worldwide. About 1,000 meals a day, mostly Indian, fly out of London aboard Air India jumbo jets. It is interesting to note that there is no difference in quality between the food in first, club or economy classes. All that varies is the way the food is served (on plastic in economy, silver service in first). Here is a first-class curry dish from Air India's restaurant in the sky.

$1\frac{1}{2}$ lb (675 g) small new
   potatoes, scrubbed

2 tablespoons tandoori
   marinade

2 tablespoons ghee

8 tablespoons curry gravy

1 tablespoon curry masala
   paste

4–6 tomatoes, puréed

2 tablespoons tomato
   ketchup

1 tablespoon chopped fresh
   coriander leaves

salt to taste

3 tablespoons single cream

Spices 1

2 teaspoons cummin seeds

2 teaspoons mustard seeds

Spices 2

2 teaspoons garam masala

2 teaspoons dry fenugreek
   leaf

1   Leave the skins on the potatoes, but scrape them a little to help the marinade adhere. Rub in the marinade, coating well. Leave to stand for up to 6 hours.

2   Preheat the oven to 325°F/160°C/Gas 3. Place the potatoes and spare marinade on to a baking tray, and bake for 15–20 minutes (depending on potato size).

3   Meanwhile heat the ghee and stir-fry **Spices 1** for 1 minute, then the curry gravy for 3 minutes, and the paste for 2 minutes. Add the tomatoes and simmer for 5 minutes.

4   Add the ketchup, coriander, **Spices 2** and salt to taste. Simmer for a further 4 minutes.

5   As soon as the potatoes are baked, add them to the sauce, and bring back to a simmer. Add the cream, mix and serve fresh and hot when tender.

Serves: *4 as an accompaniment*

BHARA ALOO
Spicy Jacket Potatoes

One of India's best Indian restaurants is the **Tanjore**, *at The Taj Mahal Intercontinental Hotel, Bombay. This restaurant comes under the auspices of chef Satish Arora, whom we have met before. This time he takes the humble potato, bakes it and stuffs it with a spicy rice filling. Finally he bakes it with a cheese topping. Nowhere before have I encountered baked potato in traditional Indian cooking. This is probably because Indian cooking has evolved over the last 6,000 years without ovens, apart from the very high heat tandoor. However, the modern oven allows us to bring forward new ideas with old subjects. Chef Arora's bhara aloo can be stuffed with all sorts of fillings. Try, for example, a kebab filling (page 53) or perhaps a chicken tikka masala filling (pages 104–5). There are endless 'curry' fillings one could use, but try Chef Arora's original version first.*

4 large potatoes, around
 6 oz (175 g) each

2 tablespoons vegetable oil

2 large spring onions with
 green, trimmed and chopped

1 teaspoon garlic purée

1 teaspoon ginger purée

$\frac{1}{2}$ each red and green
 capsicum peppers,
 seeded and finely chopped

6 tablespoons cooked rice
 (leftovers are excellent)

2 fl oz (50 ml) double or
 Cornish cream

salt to taste

4 tablespoons grated
 Cheddar cheese

Spices

1 teaspoon cummin seeds,
 roasted

1 teaspoon chilli powder

1 teaspoon curry powder

1 teaspoon garam masala

1 Wash, scrub and prick the potatoes, and wrap them in tin foil.

2 In the oven, preheated to 400°F/200°C/Gas 6, bake for around 1 hour. Test that they are cooked by poking with a thin cooking knife.

3 Meanwhile, make the stuffing. Heat the oil and stir-fry the spring onions for 2 minutes, the garlic for 1 minute, the ginger for 1 minute and the **Spices** for 1 minute. Add the capsicum peppers and stir-fry for a further 3–4 minutes.

4 Add the rice, cream and salt, toss to mix, then take off the heat.

5 When the potatoes are cooked (keep them hot), remove the foil and cut a small slice off the top of each, and scoop most of the potato out of the skin (keep for use in another recipe). Pack the stuffing into the pocket.

6 Sprinkle the grated cheese over the potatoes and grill to melt the cheese. Serve with any curry and Indian bread.

Serves: 4 as an accompaniment

KAMAL KAKRI
Lotus Stem Curry

This unusual dish comes from Kashmir, the northern-most state of India which nestles in the western Himalayan mountains. Eaten fresh, lotus roots have a taste and texture slightly resembling the fragrant Jerusalem artichoke. Being a rhizome they transport well and can be found in specialist greengrocers from time to time. They are also available canned, but, not surprisingly, they are not as subtle in this form.

1 lb (450 g) lotus roots
4 tablespoons vegetable oil
3 teaspoons garlic purée
3 teaspoons ginger purée
½ Spanish onion, peeled and
   finely chopped
2 tomatoes, chopped
4 tablespoons chopped
   fresh coriander leaves
salt to taste

Spices 1
2 teaspoons cummin seeds

Spices 2
1 teaspoon turmeric
1 teaspoon chilli powder
2 teaspoons garam masala

1 Wash, scrape and trim the lotus roots. Cut into small cubes then boil in water until tender. Times vary according to the density of the particular root. If using canned, cube, wash and keep aside.
2 Heat the oil and add **Spices 1**. When they crackle, add the garlic and ginger purées, and stir-fry for 1 minute.
3 Add the onion and stir-fry until golden (about 5 minutes).
4 Add **Spices 2**, tomato, lotus and coriander leaves. Simmer for about 10 minutes, then salt to taste.

Serves: 4 as an accompaniment

TARKA CHANA DHAL
Chickpeas in Spicy Lentil Purée

Like many people in southern India, I find dhal and plain rice not only filling and very tasty, but able to supply all the protein (from the lentils) and roughage (from the rice) that I need. I also enjoy chickpeas (chana). The idea of combining the two came to me one day and as far as I know it is an original recipe. It is easy to make, except that the chana requires a long soaking time. You can get around that by using a can or, as I do, by preparing a large batch of chana (a 500 g packet or two) at a time. Simply boil it and, when cooked, cool under a cold tap, then strain and freeze. If you can remember, take from the freezer before the chickpeas are rock hard, and shake them around to separate them, so that, like peas, they are individually frozen and you can scoop out exactly the quantity you need. This dish freezes well too.

4 oz (100 g) kabli chana (chickpeas)	2 teaspoons cummin seeds
8 oz (225 g) masoor dhal (red lentils)	2 teaspoons garlic purée
2 tablespoons ghee or vegetable oil	6 tablespoons onion purée
	1 tablespoon curry paste
	salt to taste

1 Soak the chickpeas overnight to allow them to swell and soften. Strain and rinse well. Boil up at least 2 pints (1.2 litres) water. Add the chickpeas and simmer for 45 minutes. (If that sounds as bad as a workout in the gym, you can use a can of chana adding them complete with their gravy at stage 4.)

2 The masoor also needs soaking, but only for an hour or so. Then strain and rinse. Boil up $\frac{3}{4}$ pint (450 ml) water (or stock for best taste). Add the masoor and cook for 30 minutes, stirring from time to time. The water should absorb into the lentils to produce a creamy purée.

3 Meanwhile heat the oil and fry the cummin, then the garlic and the onion for 1 minute each.

4 When the masoor is cooked, add the onion mixture and the chana, and heat. When hot, add the curry paste and mix in well. Taste and salt as needed. This dish is better cooked early on — it will keep warm for ages — or can be reheated. Make a larger quantity for freezing.

Serves: *4 as an accompaniment*

8
RICE & BREAD

The seeds of certain grasses such as barley, corn, millet, oats, rye, wheat and rice have become 'essential' or 'staple' foods. Rice is the best-known partner to curry, but not all the peoples of India regard rice as their staple.

Wheat is used to make bread, which is eaten instead of rice as an accompaniment to curry.

Rice needs a combination of fresh water and humidity to succeed in widespread cultivation. It requires careful irrigation and thrives along the fertile areas on either side of rivers. Rice grows in many regions of India, especially in the foothills of the Himalayas, in the basins of the great rivers – and all around the southern coastal tributary areas. Rice is virtually the sole staple food in Bangladesh, Burma, Thailand, Malaysia and Indonesia.

There are thousands of species of rice, but the one name which matters in curry cooking is basmati. It is a long-grained rice which when cooked has outstanding fragrance and texture.

Wheat grows in the hardier, drier parts of India, where rice does not grow. It thrives in central and north-western India, Nepal, Pakistan, Afghanistan and all lands west, and does not grow in any of the curry lands to the east. The wheat-eating areas of India include Hyderabad, Lucknow, the Punjab and Gujerat.

The breads of the sub-continent use a hard, finely-milled wholemeal flour called *ata,* or *chupatti* flour.

PLAIN BOILED RICE

This is the quickest way to cook rice, and it can be ready to serve in just 15 minutes from the water boiling. Two factors are crucial for this method to work perfectly. Firstly the rice must be basmati rice. Patna or long-grained, quick-cook or other rices, will require different timings and will have neither the texture nor the fragrance of basmati. Secondly, it is one of the few recipes in this book which requires precision timing. It is essential that for its few minutes on the boil you concentrate on it or else it may over-cook and become stodgy.

A 3 oz (75 g) portion of dry rice provides an ample helping per person: 2 oz (50 g) will be a smaller but adequate portion. To spice the plain cooked rice, see the next two recipes.

> **8–12 oz (225–350 g)**
>   **basmati or other long-**
>   **grained rice**
> **2–3 pints (1.2–1.8 litres)**
>   **water**

1 Pick through the rice to remove grit and particles.

2 Boil the water. It is not necessary to salt it.

3 While it is heating up, rinse the rice briskly with fresh cold water until most of the starch is washed out. Run hot tap water through the rice at the final rinse. This minimises the temperature reduction of the boiling water when you put the rice into it.

4 When the water is boiling properly, put the rice into the pan. Start timing. Put the lid on the pan until the water comes back to the boil then remove.

5 It takes 8–10 minutes from the start. Stir frequently.

6 After about 6 minutes, taste a few grains. As soon as the centre is no longer brittle, but still has a good *al dente* bite to it, strain off the water. It should seem slightly *undercooked*.

7 Shake off all excess water, then place the strainer on to a dry teatowel which will help remove the last of the water.

8 After a minute place the rice in a pre-warmed serving dish. You can serve it now or put it into a low oven or warming drawer for about half an hour minimum. As it dries, the grains will separate and become fluffy. It can be held in the warmer for several hours if needed.

Serves: 4

SPICED RICE

1 For even tastier rice you can add coconut powder and ground almonds as on page 149.

2 You can also spice it as for the lemon rice method in the recipe on page 150.

3 If you want to achieve the different coloured grains that restaurants do, you have to use food colouring powder (see below). The best colour is sunset yellow, and to achieve it, simply sprinkle a tiny tip of the teaspoonful on top of the rice *before* it goes in the warmer. Do not stir it in. Allow it 30 minutes to soak in and *then* stir. You'll get a mixture of coloured grains from deep to pale yellow mixed in with white, and very attractive it looks too. If you wish to go 'multi-coloured', with yellow, red and/or green, separate the rice into three portions, colour as stated, and keep separate in warmer. Mix together after half an hour.

Serves: 4 with moderate appetites

QUICK PULLAO RICE

This and the following recipe are spicings for plain boiled rice which each only take 5 minutes – so you can be ready with a perfect pullao or lemon rice in as little as 20 minutes from the start.

1 dessertspoon butter ghee	**Spices**
1 recipe plain boiled rice	1 teaspoon fennel seeds
1 dessertspoon coconut powder	1 teaspoon black cummin seeds
1 dessertspoon ground almonds	
a pinch of sunset yellow food colouring (optional)	

1 Heat the ghee and stir-fry the **Spices** for 30 seconds.
2 Add the other ingredients, and stir in until hot.
3 Serve immediately.

Serves: 4

QUICK LEMON RICE

1 dessertspoon mustard oil	*Spices*
1 recipe plain boiled rice	1 teaspoon mustard seeds
2 tablespoons fried cashew nuts	1 teaspoon sesame seeds
1 tablespoon coconut powder	1 teaspoon turmeric
juice of 2 lemons	6 curry leaves, fresh or dry

1 Cook exactly as in the previous recipe.

Serves: 4

RICE BY ABSORPTION

Cooking rice by a pre-measured ratio of rice to water which is all absorbed into the rice is undoubtedly the best way to do it. Provided that you use basmati rice, the finished grains are longer, thinner and much more fragrant and flavourful than they are after boiling.

The method is easy, but many cookbooks make it sound far too complicated. Instructions invariably state that you must use a tightly lidded pot and precise water quantity and heat levels, and never lift the lid during the boiling process, etc, etc. However, I lift the lid, I might stir the rice, and I've even cooked rice by absorption without a lid. Also, if I've erred on the side of too little water, I've added a bit during 'the boil'. (Too much water is an unresolvable problem). It's all naughty, rule-breaking stuff, but it still seems to work.

Another factor, always omitted in other people's books, is the time factor. They all say or imply that rice must be served as soon as 'the boil' is completed. This causes stress to the cook who believes that there is no margin of error in time and method. In reality, the longer you give the rice to absorb the water/steam, the fluffier and more fragrant it will be. So it can be cooked well in advance of being required for serving. For after the initial 'boil' and 10-minute simmer the rice is quite sticky, and it needs to 'relax'. After 30 minutes it can be served and is fluffy, but it can be kept in a warm place for much longer — improving in fluffiness all the time. This is the way the restaurants do it. They cook in bulk using up to $8\frac{3}{4}$ lb (4 kg) rice (around 60 portions) at a time in huge aluminium saucepans. They follow this recipe exactly (the *timings do not change, no matter how much rice is being used). They cook their rice at the end of the lunch session, put it in a very low heat oven, and by the opening of business at 6pm it's perfect and, kept warm in the oven, lasts the whole evening.*

Cooking rice does need practice. You may need one or two goes at it. Here are some tips for the newcomer:

1 Choose a pan, preferably with a lid, which can be used both on the stove and in the oven. Until you have had lots of practice, always use the same pan, so that you become familiar with it.

2 Keep a good eye on the clock. The timing of 'the boil' is important or you'll burn the bottom of the rice.

3 Use basmati rice.

4 If you intend to let the rice cool down for serving later, or the next day, or to freeze it, do not put it in the warmer. It is better slightly undercooked for these purposes.

After a few goes at this you'll do it without thinking. Here is my foolproof method. The full complement of spices listed below gives a really tasty rice. You can omit some if you don't have them to hand. Some restaurants just use the fennel and black cummin seeds and these are very fragrant. If you don't like chewy spices omit or remove the cloves, bay, cassia, etc.

20 fl oz (570 ml) water, *or*, for tastier results (the way the restaurants do it), 10 fl oz (285 ml) milk, plus 10 fl oz (285 ml) water

1 tablespoon butter ghee

Spices

4 green cardamoms

4 cloves

2 inch (5 cm) piece cassia bark

2 bay leaves

1 teaspoon fennel seeds

$\frac{1}{2}$ teaspoon black cummin seeds

1 brown cardamom

2 star anises

Note: 10 oz (285 g) is 2 teacups of dry rice, and 20 fl oz is about $1\frac{1}{3}$ volume of water to 1 of rice. This 10:20 (2 teacups: 1 pint) combination is easy to remember, but do step up or step down the quantities as required in proportion.

For small appetites, for instance, use:
   8 oz (225 g) rice: 16 fl oz (450 ml) water
For large appetites:
   12 oz (350 g) rice: 24 fl oz (685 ml) water

1 Soak the rice in water for about half an hour.

2 Rinse it until the rinse water is more or less clear, then strain.

3 Boil up the water (or water and milk).

4 In a saucepan (as heavy as possible, and with a lid), or a casserole dish at least twice the volume of the strained rice, heat the ghee then fry the **Spices** for 30 seconds.

5 Add the rice and stir-fry, ensuring the oil coats the rice, and it heats up.

6 Then add the boiled water (or water and milk), and stir in well. Put the lid on, keep the heat high and leave well alone for 8 minutes.

7 Inspect. Has the liquid absorbed on top? If not, replace the lid and leave for 2 more minutes. If and when it has, stir the rice well, ensuring that it is not sticking to the bottom. Now taste. It should not be brittle in the middle. If it is, add a little more water and keep on high heat a little longer.

8 Place the saucepan or casserole into an oven preheated to its very lowest setting. The longer you leave the rice, the more separate the grains will be. An hour is fine, but it will be quite safe and happy left for several hours.

RESTAURANT-STYLE BIRIANI/PULLAO

I do not know of many restaurants which make biriani or pullao in the traditional manner. It's not that they are incapable of doing so: it's because, firstly, it takes a fair while to cook them correctly; secondly, if the dishes are not ordered on the night they would have to be scrapped. So the restaurants 'fake' it.

Biriani and pullao, restaurant style, consist of pre-cooked meat, chicken, king prawn or vegetable, dry-fried with a little curry gravy into which pre-cooked pullao rice is stir-fried. Pullao is served at this point in the preparation. Biriani sometimes has a separate onion and whole spice tarka stir-fried in or applied as a garnish along with fried egg, almonds, tomato and sultanas; it is normally served with curry gravy (a combination of a quick fry-up of some spices and curry masala gravy as on page 30).

These methods work passably well, but the correct method of making pullaos and birianis in the following recipes are worth trying at home where you'll capture the maximum flavours by using absorption techniques.

This recipe is for a typical biriani as served, for example, at the popular **Agra Indian***, 32 East Street, Warminster, Wiltshire.*

1 tablespoon ghee or oil	**Garnish**
6 tablespoons sliced onion	fried egg or omelette
1 teaspoon curry paste	whole fried almonds
2 tablespoons curry masala gravy	fresh tomato slices
	sultanas
8 oz (225 g) pre-cooked meat	desiccated coconut
1 lb (450 g) pre-cooked pullao rice	

1 Heat the oil, and stir-fry the onion until golden brown (5–8 minutes). Remove half for garnish.

2 Add the paste to the onion in the pan and fry for 1 minute, then add the gravy. Heat until simmering, then add the meat, which should 'soak' up the sauce.

3 When it does, add the rice. Mix well – but gently – and serve when hot, or keep in a warmer until you are ready.

Serves: 4

AKHNI PULLAO
Spicy Rice with Chickpeas

When The Curry Club launched its 1986 Good Curry Guide – its guide to the best 700 curry restaurants in Britain – I invited 10 of the top 30 restaurants to come to London to appear at our press launch party and to cook just one dish each for the 250 assembled guests and journalists. The restaurant which came the furthest was **Lancers**, *5 Hamilton Place, Edinburgh and this is the recipe for the dish they served.*

8–12 oz (225–350 g) basmati rice

4 dessertspoons butter ghee

1 inch (2.5 cm) piece fresh ginger, sliced

$\frac{1}{2}$ Spanish onion, peeled and chopped

$\frac{1}{4}$ green capsicum pepper, seeded and sliced

2–4 fresh green chillies, chopped (to taste)

1 tablespoon chopped fresh coriander leaves

2 oz (50 g) chickpeas, cooked

salt to taste

Spices

4 green cardamoms

4 cloves

2 inch (5 cm) piece cassia bark

2 bay leaves

$\frac{1}{2}$ teaspoon turmeric

Garnish

8–10 pistachio nuts, sliced

1 Soak the rice for 30 minutes, then rinse.

2 Warm a lidded casserole and heat the ghee. Stir-fry the ginger for 1 minute then the onions for 3 minutes. Add the green peppers, chillies and **Spices**. Cook for 3 minutes, and when soft, add the coriander and chickpeas.

3 Stir in the rice. Add boiling water to cover the rice by about one-third of its depth, and bring to the boil. When the rice rises, cover the pot, turn down to simmer and leave alone until the water has been absorbed by the rice (about 10 minutes).

4 Place the pot in a preheated oven at its lowest heat for at least 30 minutes.

5 After this remove the rice and stir it with a fork to aerate it and let the steam escape. Serve with a garnish of pistachio nuts.

Serves: 4

KEDGEREE
Rice with Lentils

The British in India produced a unique range of dishes, Anglo-Indian cuisine, now sadly becoming gradually forgotten. Many of these dishes were adaptations of long-established Indian dishes and one of these, which still remains in both forms, is kedgeree or kitchri. *The former is the Anglo-Indian version of a rice dish, a sort of pullao which contains smoked haddock, boiled egg and pepper.*

The original Indian dish is Gujerati in origin and is a mixture of rice and lentils. One of the few restaurants to serve it is one of Wales' best establishments – the **Viceroy of India**, *50 St Helen's Road, Swansea.*

8–12 oz (225–350 g)
  basmati rice
2 oz (50 g) masoor dhal (red
  lentils)
2 tablespoons butter ghee
1 teaspoon garlic purée
$\frac{1}{2}$ Spanish onion, peeled and
  thinly sliced

Spices
1 teaspoon white cummin
  seeds
1 teaspoon black mustard
  seeds

1 Soak the rice for 30 minutes, then rinse.

2 Heat the ghee, and stir-fry the **Spices**, garlic and onion for 5 minutes.

3 Boil the lentils in water (page 96). Do so completely, until they are soft, if adding to boiled rice; cook only half-way if adding to rice cooked by the absorption method.

4 If boiling the rice, add the fried items and the lentils after it has been strained, mixing it well.

5 If cooking the rice by absorption, add it to the ghee-fried ingredients, along with the half-cooked lentils, and proceed as on pages 150–1.

Serves: 4

NAVRATTAN PULLAO

*This rice dish has a combination of nine vegetables, fruits and nuts. You can cut down on the number of ingredients, or you can add more or alternatives. It is a very festive and decorative dish with wide appeal. The edible silver (or gold) leaf garnish makes an interesting talking point (page 157). I met this particular recipe in India, but a similar dish is to be found at the **Laguna**, 77 Narborough Road, Leicester.*

8–12 oz (225–350 g)
  basmati rice

6 tablespoons butter ghee

8 small cauliflower florets,
  blanched

1–2 carrots, diced and
  blanched

1 courgette, diced and
  blanched

2 tablespoons green peas,
  blanched

1 tablespoon grapes,
  seedless preferably

1 slice pineapple, diced

$\frac{1}{2}$ apple, diced

1 tablespoon cashew nuts

1 tablespoon almonds

1 tablespoon *chirongee*
  seeds

$\frac{1}{2}$ teaspoon salt

Spices

3 cloves

2 green cardamoms

1 blade mace

Garnish

rosewater

4 sheets silver leaf (*vark*)

1 Soak the rice for 30 minutes, then rinse well.

2 Heat the ghee, and stir-fry the **Spices** for 1 minute.

3 If boiling the rice, add the spices, vegetables and other ingredients after it has been strained, mixing in well. Place in the oven for a short while.

4 If cooking the rice by absorption, add the rice to the **Spices** and cook as on page 151. Mix in the vegetables and other ingredients once it is cooked and then place in the oven.

5 Sprinkle just before serving with the rosewater, and garnish with *vark*.

Serves: 4

NOOR MAHAL BIRIANI

This dish originated in the city of Lucknow. It is a rich and colourful dish — a meal in itself — and is typical of the good-living days of Lucknow in the early nineteenth century. This biriani recipe is from the Mughal Sheraton's fine **Taj-Banu** *restaurant. A similar dish is found at the* **Kohinoor** *restaurant, 88 Liverpool Road, Preston, Lancs, where it is called Persian Royal Lamb Biriani.*

The colours are achieved by colouring the cashew nuts, and the edible silver and/or gold leaf adornments (vark) are said to have been created by the chefs of the happy-go-lucky Nawabs, the rulers of the day, to reflect the colours of the local attire. To this day the saris of the area are more often than not traditionally red, green or yellow with an immense amount of gold or silver filigree work on them.

The tradition of garnishing biriani dishes, as well as fudge-like sweets (barfi), goes back inevitably to the Moghul emperors. They took great delight in displaying their wealth, and eating it. At certain banquets, it is said, rice dishes contained pearls and 'cloves' made from solid gold, which the recipient was supposed to return to the emperor with due thanks upon finding it in his serving. Rumour has it that certain guests of the emperor knowingly swallowed these trinkets so as to be able to smuggle them out of the royal presence and recover them later. Be that as it may, the silver and gold leaf was for eating, and the tradition has been carried on to this day. I have seen silver leaf being made in a small workshop in Hyderabad. The craftsman takes a small nugget of silver, then places it in a leather pouch. He proceeds to beat the pouch with a special hammer until the silver is thinner than cigarette papers and about 5 inches (12.5 cm) square. It is then placed between sheets of tissue paper (this craftsman was using old railway timetables) and sold in lots of 100.

To use, carefully peel off the outer piece of tissue paper and discard, ensuring the silver or gold leaf has not stuck to it. Then lift up the next sheet of tissue and dab the leaf on to the hot food. Do not finger it, or it will disintegrate. Supplies are very hard to obtain in the West, and I have been advised by health officers that it is common practice to adulterate the silver with aluminium. The leaf sold by The Curry Club is purchased in Bombay by ourselves from the city's most reputable hotel- and sweet-shop supplier.

One final word about vark . . . it is said that it is an aphrodisiac. It is not for me to confirm or deny this, but it will certainly make an interesting talking point if you use it for your next party! (see overleaf)

Noor mahal biriani

8–12 oz (225–350 g)
  basmati rice

4 oz (100 g) minced lamb or
  beef

2 oz (50 g) lean lamb or
  beef, cubed

salt to taste

1 teaspoon garam masala

3 tablespoons garlic purée

6 tablespoons butter ghee

8 tablespoons onion purée

2 teaspoons ginger purée

3 oz (75 ml) natural yoghurt

$\frac{1}{2}$ teaspoon paprika

$\frac{1}{2}$ teaspoon ground black
  pepper

akhni stock or water

Spices (roasted and ground)

4 inch (10 cm) piece cassia
  bark

$\frac{1}{2}$ nutmeg

6 cloves

6 green cardamoms

Garnish

2 oz (50 g) raw cashew nuts

red, green and yellow food
  colouring (optional)

some fresh red cherries (or
  bottled Maraschinos)

4 sheets of silver leaf (*vark*)

1 Wash the rice well and soak in cold water for 30 minutes, then drain.

2 Mix the minced lamb with some salt, the garam masala and 1 teaspoon of the garlic until blended well. Form into small koftas (balls).

3 Heat the ghee in a large, heavy saucepan and fry the onion, remaining garlic and the ginger until golden.

4 Add the cubes of lamb and fry, stirring, until the colour changes.

5 Stir in the yoghurt mixed with 6–8 fl oz (175–250 ml) water, some salt, the paprika and pepper. Cover and cook until the lamb is half done (about 15 minutes).

6 Now add the *koftas*, and continue cooking until the lamb is tender, stirring occasionally. If there is too much liquid in the pan, uncover and cook, stirring, until it has almost all evaporated.

7 Now add the rice, the **Spices** and enough stock or water to cover the rice by one-third. Bring to the boil, cover with a well fitting lid, turn heat very low and cook for 25 minutes without lifting the lid or stirring, until all the liquid has been absorbed by the rice. Uncover and allow steam to escape for a couple of minutes.

8 While the rice is cooking, boil the garnish cashew nuts separately in water to which some food colouring has been added (a few minutes). Colour some cashews red, some green and some yellow. Ground turmeric may be used for the yellow colouring or, if preferred, simply fry the nuts in oil until golden brown.

9 When the biriani is ready, garnish with nuts, cherries and vark. Serve piping hot as a main dish in its own right — you won't really need another meat or veg dish — with gravy, bread, chutneys and papadoms.

Serves: *4*

NAAN BREAD
Tandoori Leavened White Flour Bread

Naan is a huge, light, fluffy and chewy flat bread, made from white flour lightly leavened and spiced. It's cooked traditionally by hanging in the tandoor, which accounts for the tear-drop shape, but in this method it's grilled. This recipe is from the **Shalimar**, *56 Athol Street, Perth, Tayside.*

2 oz (50 g) fresh yeast, *or* 3 tablespoons natural yoghurt

lukewarm water

1½ lb (675 g) strong white plain flour, *or* 12 oz (340 g) strong white plain flour *plus* 12 oz

(340 g) white chupatti (*ata*) flour

melted butter ghee

Spices

2 teaspoons sesame seeds

2 teaspoons wild onion seeds

1 Melt the fresh yeast in a little warm water until it has dissolved.

2 Put the flour in a warmed bowl, make a well in the centre, and pour in the melted yeast or the yoghurt.

3 Gently mix into the flour, and add enough warm water to make a firm dough.

4 Remove from the bowl and knead on a floured board until well combined. Return to the bowl and leave in a warm place for a couple of hours to rise.

5 Your dough, when risen, should double in size. It should be bubbly, stringy and like elastic.

6 'Knock back' the dough by kneading it down to its original size. Add the **Spices**.

7 Divide the dough into four pieces and roll each into an oblong shape. The tear-drop shape comes from the dough being hung inside the tandoor, and if you want that shape roll accordingly.

8 Preheat the grill to its maximum temperature. Place some foil on the grill pan rack to catch drips. Put the *naan* on the foil and the pan at the half way slot. Brush one side of each naan with melted ghee and place under the grill. Watch them cook (they can *over* cook and burn very easily). As the first side develops brown patches, remove and turn. Brush more ghee on the turned side and replace under the heat. Serve immediately.

Makes: *4 naans*

KEEMA NAAN
Mince-Stuffed Tandoori Bread

As with most Indian breads, the naan can be stuffed or folded around a filling. The filling is based on a traditional mince (keema), but in this case it is first tandoori-baked in a flat disc. This is a recent discovery by the restaurateurs and is rightfully a firm favourite (it's much easier to do). Here is the method used by the **Simla**, *48 Weyhill, Haslemere, Surrey — which just happens to be my very excellent local.*

**approx. 6 oz (175 g) raw
   sheek kebab (see page
   53)**
1 naan recipe (page 160)

1 Divide the kebab mix into four, and flatten each into a 4 inch (10 cm) oval disc.
2 Either fry the discs on a *tava* or bake in the oven at 325°F/160°C/Gas 3 for 10–15 minutes. Allow to cool.
4 Make up the naan dough as in the previous recipe. At stage 7, carefully enclose the kebab disc inside the dough and roll out. Carry on with stage 8.

Makes: *4 naans*

Previous Page
Accompaniments: *Pullao Rice* (**pages 152–3**), *Tarka Chana Dhal* (**page 146**), *Naan Bread* (**page 160**) (**with various chutneys and accompaniments**).

Left
The Sweet Trolley: *Kesari Shrikhand* (**page 176**), *Coconut Pancakes* (**pages 174–5**), *Moira Banana* (**page 179**).

ONION KULCHA
Leavened White Flour Bread

This speciality bread from central India is made — in this recipe from the **Bombay** *restaurant, 43 Timberhill, Norwich — from the same dough as naan bread. The traditional shape is square with a decorative cross pattern made with the fingertips. This version has an onion stuffing.*

> 1 lb (450 g) naan bread
>   dough (pages 160–1)
>   incorporating 2
>   tablespoons melted
>   butter ghee
> 4 tablespoons sliced
>   onions, fried in ghee until
>   brown

1 Divide the dough into four balls.

2 Roll each out roughly and place equal amounts of cold onion in each. Fold the dough over the onion. Re-roll to a square of about 6 inches (15 cm).

3 Mark a cross shape, dotting with a finger, if you like, then grill as with naan.

Makes: 4 kulchas

PARATHA
Unleavened Wheatflour Layered Bread

Parathas are the Indian version of layered bread (a sort of puff pastry). When shallow-fried they should end up crispy on the outside yet soft and 'melt-in-the-mouth'. Note the 'snake' method to achieve the layering which is used by just about every restaurant. Stuffing is optional, and this plain version is from **The Raj Belash**, *36 Hills Road, Cambridge, Cambs. A mint or methi version can be found at* **Veeraswamy's**, *99 Regent Street, London W1. Also from Veeraswamy's is besan lacha paratha, an unusual paratha which is an equal mixture of gram flour (besan) and ata flour. Follow the same method exactly as for ordinary parathas.*

1 lb (450 g) ata *or*
   wholemeal flour
melted butter ghee

1 Mix the flour and 2 tablespoons of the ghee with enough tepid
   water to make a soft dough.

2 Divide the dough into four. Roll each piece into a long sausage then
   flatten it into a strip about 12 × 3 inches (30 × 7.5 cm). Apply melted
   ghee to the strip, then roll it up from the long side to make a snake.
   Coil the snake around itself into a shape like a three-dimensional
   ice-cream cone, narrow point up.

3 Sprinkle extra flour on the cone then gently push it down with the
   hand and then roll it out to an 8 inch (20 cm) disc.

4 Heat 2 tablespoons ghee on a *tava* and fry the paratha until it is
   hot. Lift it out with tongs. Add more ghee and repeat on the other
   side.

Makes: 4 *parathas*

PURI
Deep-Fried Unleavened Bread

*The puri uses the same ata flour dough as the paratha. Serve with the dishes
of your choice. It goes particularly well with Prawn patia puri on page 59.*

**8 oz (225 g) ata or
   wholemeal flour**
1 tablespoon butter ghee
**6–8 fl oz (175–250 ml) hot
   water**

$\frac{1}{4}$ **teaspoon salt**
**vegetable oil for deep-
   frying**

1 Make a soft dough from the flour, ghee, water and salt. Let it stand
   to soften and absorb fully for half an hour.

2 Divide into four then divide each four into four – it's the easiest
   way of getting 16 similar sized pieces.

3 Shape each into a ball then roll out to 4 inch (10 cm) discs.

4 Preheat oil or a deep-fryer to 375°F/190°C, and immerse one disc
   in the oil at a time. It should puff up quickly. Turn when it does,
   and remove after 30 seconds. Serve at once.

Makes: 16 *puris*

LOOCHI
Deep-Fried Unleavened White Flour Bread

From the North-West Frontier, the loochi is a strong white flour version of the previous puri recipe. Simply make with 8 oz (225 g) strong white flour in place of the ata or wholemeal flour. You'll find loochi at the **Taj Mahal**, *6 Baddow Road, Chelmsford, Essex.*

BHATURA
Leavened White Flour and Semolina Bread

This Punjabi style of bread uses approximately two parts of white flour and one part of semolina (ground durum wheat flour) to produce an interesting texture. Traditionally bhatura are eaten with chana (page 52), but they go nicely with everything. You will find bhatura at **The Days of the Raj**, *51 Dale End, Birmingham.*

5 oz (150 g) strong white
   plain flour

3 oz (75 g) semolina

2 teaspoons natural
   yoghurt

$\frac{1}{2}$ teaspoon salt

1 Mix the flour, semolina, yoghurt and salt with enough warm water to make a dough as for puri.

2 Leave it to stand in a warm place to rise (about a couple of hours).

3 Roll out to 4 inch (10 cm) discs, and deep-fry in hot oil as for puri until golden. Shake off excess oil, and serve at once.

Makes: 16 bhaturas

MAKKI-KI-ROTI
Cornflour Bread

Kashmir, high in the western Himalayas, is a rice-eating area, and wheat eating was, until very recent times, unknown. Cornflour is the Kashmiri alternative to wheat.

8 oz (225 g) cornflour
1 teaspoon salt
$\frac{1}{2}$ teaspoon chilli powder
butter ghee

1 Mix the cornflour, salt and chilli powder with enough water to make a soft dough. Let it stand for half an hour.
2 Divide the dough into four, and roll each piece out to form a large disc about 8 inches (20 cm) in diameter.
3 Dry-cook it on a tava or griddle pan. As it flecks to brown turn over and do the same to the other side.
4 Serve spread with ghee.

Serves: *4*

9
ACCOMPANIMENTS

Indian food is a fabulous combination of rich creamy curries with fluffy rice or tasty breads, but it is the chutney and pickle dishes which are the perfect and indispensable accompaniment to the Indian meal. The tangy fresh salads in this chapter are very easy to make and are one of the few raw vegetable intakes (therefore containing vitamin C) in the Indian repertoire. Being tangy, they activate the salivary glands and improve the digestive process.

So too do bottled pickles, and there are dozens of very good varieties on the market. Most use lime, chilli or mango, and they can vary enormously from very sour to very sweet (mango), and very mild to very hot. In the companion volume to this, *The Curry Club Indian Restaurant Cookbook*, I give recipes for several of these pickles, but as they are time-consuming to make and require quite long maturation periods, most restaurants buy them in.

ONION SALAD

The standard fresh chutney at the curry house. Make this early so that the onion marinates and softens. Cover the bowl with clingfilm and keep in the fridge.

$\frac{1}{2}$ **Spanish onion, peeled and**   **juice of $\frac{1}{2}$ lemon**
    thinly sliced   **a pinch of dried mint**

1 Simply mix all the ingredients together.

INDIAN SALAD

This delightful combination of taste and colour is served as a starter or accompaniment dish at **Veeraswamy**, *Swallow Street, London W1.*

8 walnuts, halved   **4 oz (100 g) beansprouts**
6 radishes, sliced   **juice of 2 lemons**
1 tablespoon raisins   **1 teaspoon dried mint**
3 inch (7.5 cm) piece   **salt to taste**
   cucumber, sliced

1 Simply mix all the ingredients together.

CACHUMBER PALAVA

A simple and colourful chutney. Serve fresh.

2 small pink onions, peeled   **$\frac{1}{2}$ teaspoon dried mint**
   and chopped   **1 tablespoon chopped**
1 teaspoon chopped fresh   **'black' capsicum pepper**
   coriander leaves   **$\frac{1}{4}$ lime**

1 Simply mix all the ingredients together, serving the lime wedge on top.

CACHUMBER PUNJABI

Another version of the previous recipe.

½ Spanish onion, peeled and
  chopped
1 teaspoon chopped fresh
  coriander leaves

1 teaspoon each of chopped
  red and yellow capsicum
  peppers
1 green chilli, chopped
  (optional)

1 Simply mix all the ingredients together.

COCONUT CHUTNEY

Originating from South India, but delicious as a chutney with any dish. It's easy to make, and very tasty.

2 teaspoons mustard oil
2 teaspoons sesame seeds
1 teaspoon black mustard
  seeds
3 tablespoons desiccated
  coconut

1 tablespoon coconut
  powder
milk
a pinch of salt

1 Heat the oil, and fry the seeds for 1 minute. Cool.
2 Mix the two coconuts with enough milk to form a stiff paste. Mix
     with the spices and salt. Serve cold.

IMLI
Tamarind Chutney

*This is a very tasty chutney — a dip really. Pity that so few restaurants make it, but it does take time to make the tamarind juice. Luckily, the Curry Club's best local, **The Simla,** 84 Weyhill, Haslemere, Surrey, make it and it's perfect for dipping papadoms into! Freeze any spare.*

6 fl oz (175 ml) tamarind
    purée
brown sugar to taste
salt to taste
1 teaspoon curry masala
    paste

1 Simply mix all the ingredients together.

THAI CUCUMBER

A tangy chutney from Thailand which goes well with Indian food too.

4 inch (10 cm) piece
    cucumber, quartered and
    chopped
1 spring onion, trimmed
    and chopped
1 tablespoon chopped fresh
    coriander leaves

1 teaspoon sesame seeds
3–4 fl oz (85–120 ml) any
    vinegar
1 teaspoon white sugar
salt to taste

1 Simply mix all the ingredients together.

WHITE RADISH (MOOLI) CHUTNEY

Fresh, tangy and quick to make, this chutney goes well with all dishes.

> 1 medium size mooli about
>   8 oz (225 g)
> 1 tablespoon white spirit
>   vinegar
> 1 tablespoon curry masala
>   paste

1 Wash the mooli, scrape the outside clean, and cut off top and bottom. Shred it in a food processor or a grater into thin strips.

2 Mix the vinegar and paste then combine with the mooli.

3 Serve cold and fresh. Either freeze any leftovers or cook it into your next curry.

SAG PACHADI
Spinach Chutney

This is a kind of raita (a yoghurt-based salad) from the southern tip of India. Make it as thick or thin as you like and serve it as an accompaniment, hot or cold.

> 1 lb (450 g) fresh spinach
>   (or frozen)
> 1 tablespoon cummin seeds
> 2 tablespoons mustard oil
> 1 tablespoon mustard seeds
>
> 10 oz (275 g) natural
>   yoghurt, strained
> akhni stock or milk if
>   necessary

1 Thoroughly wash the fresh spinach, then coarsely chop it. Boil for 3 minutes and strain.

2 Heat a dry pan on the stove and 'roast' the cummin seeds.

3 Heat the oil and fry the mustard seeds until they pop. Add the spinach well off the heat, then the yoghurt. Heat gently (if you wish to serve the dish hot) and stir frequently to prevent curdling.

4 Add the roasted cummin. If you want a runnier dish simply add stock or milk to the consistency.

Serves: *4 as an accompaniment*

Mint Raita
Yoghurt Chutney

A deliciously cool and cooling accompaniment. It should be chilled and served within the hour.

1 cup plain yoghurt

1 teaspoon finely chopped
   fresh mint

salt and pepper

Spices (optional)

$\frac{1}{2}$ teaspoon chilli powder

$\frac{1}{2}$ teaspoon garam masala

Garnish

fresh chopped coriander
pinch of nutmeg

1   Drain any excess liquid off the yoghurt, then beat with a whisk or fork, rotary or electric beater until smooth. There should be no 'grains'.

2   Add mint, salt and pepper plus the *spices* if used.

3   Serve chilled within the hour. Garnish prior to serving with fresh coriander and nutmeg.

10
DESSERTS

The puddings and sweetmeats of India are quite frankly very limited in range, and they are an acquired taste. They are usually very sweet indeed, very sticky and most are milk based.

In this chapter I have reduced the sugar levels to a more acceptable amount (you can always add more) which I find brings out the delightful (once acquired) tastes of the spicing, usually green cardamom and saffron.

I urge you to try Indian desserts from time to time, but if you want something lighter, India's national fruit — the mango — is ideal.

FIRNI
Spicy White Custard

*Firni is typical of the Indian pudding, and it consists of milk, cornflour, sugar, nuts and spices. It is served cold. A variation of this recipe is Faloda. It can be found at the attractive **Sheik's** restaurant, Simes Street, Bradford, where they add vermicelli to the other ingredients.*

$1\frac{3}{4}$ pints (a good litre) milk

2 tablespoons cornflour or rice flour

8 fl oz (250 ml) sweetened condensed milk

$\frac{1}{4}$ teaspoon ground green cardamom

2 tablespoons milk powder

2 tablespoons ground almonds

Garnish

silver or gold leaf (page 157)

pistachio nuts, chopped

1 Make a paste from a little milk and the cornflour.
2 Heat the milk but don't boil it. Add the paste and stir until it thickens.
3 Add all the remaining ingredients and mix in gently.
4 Pour into a decorative serving bowl and place it in the fridge for at least 2 hours to thicken.
5 Garnish with silver or gold leaf and pistachio nuts.

Serves: 4

SHAHI KEER
Creamy Rice Pudding

Every year in late September a great festival is held all over India to give thanksgiving to Ganesha (the elephant god). A special sweet is prepared and eaten in celebration — kheer, basically a creamy rice pudding. One of the very few restaurants to serve this dish, which they call shahi kheer, is **Veeraswamy, 99 Regent Street, London W1.**

4 oz (100 g) round-grain pudding rice	**Garnish**
1 pint (600 ml) milk	1 tablespoon sultanas
8 fl oz (250 ml) sweetened condensed milk	1 tablespoon flaked almonds
$\frac{1}{2}$ teaspoon saffron	

1 Soak the rice in cold water for 30 minutes, then rinse.

2 Boil the rice and the milk together, then simmer, stirring from time to time, until the rice is cooked and soft (about 15 minutes).

3 Add the condensed milk and saffron. When hot serve, garnished with the sultanas and flaked almonds. It can also be served cold.

Serves: 4

COCONUT PANCAKES

It's amazing what politicians do when they want to impress each other. For years in Goa, traffic using the main road from the airport to the main town of Panjim used to drive aboard a tiny ferry to cross a wide river. In fact, it could just accommodate a standard 30-seat coach. The crossing took about 10 minutes, the queue for the ferry rather longer, but it was fun, for the tourist at any rate.

Then in 1983, India held the Commonwealth Heads of Government meeting in Goa. The Queen and Mrs Thatcher attended it along with 20 or 30 other heads of government. The setting was idyllic — the Taj Group's **Fort Aguada Holiday Resort.** *But such events spur big actions — both from the hotel group, who built 25 luxury villas with all mod. cons. to house their VIPs, and the Indian Government, who built a massive two-mile bridge over the river* so that the VIP limos would not have to queue for the ferry. Pity really – I miss that quaint bit of India. This was one of the dishes served by The Fort's chefs for the dignitaries. Alas, I have never encountered a dessert like this in any UK Indian restaurant, yet it is really very simple for anyone who can cook a pancake.

4 oz (100 g) plain white
   flour
2 oz (50 g) butter, melted
2 eggs, beaten
10 fl oz (300 ml) milk,
   warmed
1 tablespoon sugar
a few drops of vanilla
   essence
butter
lemon juice

Filling
7 oz (200 g) fresh coconut,
   grated
2 oz (50 g) jaggery or brown
   sugar
$1\frac{1}{2}$ oz (40 g) raisins
$\frac{1}{4}$ teaspoon ground cassia
   bark
$\frac{1}{4}$ teaspoon ground green
   cardamom

1 To make the pancakes, sift the flour into a bowl, and mix in the melted butter, eggs, warm milk, sugar and vanilla. Mix well. It should be of pouring consistency.
2 Mix all the filling ingredients together.
3 In a very hot tava, heat a little butter. Pour in enough batter which, when 'swilled' around the pan, makes a thin pancake. (If thin enough it won't need turning.)
4 Place some of the filling in the centre of each pancake. Roll up and keep warm. Serve with a squeeze of lemon.

Makes: *12–14 Pancakes*

KESARI SHRIKHAND
Saffron Yoghurt Syllabub

Shrikhand is incredibly easy to make, as it is virtually instant. It is light and sweetish and, being thick in texture, it is fun and elegant to serve it in stemmed wine glasses for the more elaborate occasion. You can reduce the strain of entertaining by putting the mixture into the glasses early on and holding them in the fridge until you are ready to serve. This recipe is from the famous **Tangore** *restaurant at Bombay's Taj International Hotel.*

$1\frac{1}{4}$ lb (550 g) natural
   yoghurt, strained (best
   for taste and texture)

5 fl oz (150 ml) double or
   Cornish cream

2 tablespoons ground
   almonds

3 tablespoons sugar (adjust
   up or down to taste)

1 teaspoon ground green
   cardamoms

6–10 saffron strands

Garnish

freshly grated nutmeg
pistachio nuts, chopped

1 Simply hand beat all the ingredients together.

2 After placing into serving bowls or glasses, garnish with freshly grated nutmeg and pistachio nuts.

Serves: 4

SHAHI TUKRE
Indian Bread and Butter Pudding

Don't be put off by the thought that this is a stodgy, unappealing pudding. It is in fact very Indian and when spiced with green cardamom, saffron, vanilla and rose-water and garnished with silver leaf (vark), it is one of the nicest of Indian puddings. Served cold, it can be made well in advance, which is especially useful if using it for a dinner party, and no one will guess its 'humble' and relatively inexpensive ingredients.

I first met this dish (also called Double Ka Mitha*) in Delhi, and I have since cooked it several times for up to 60 people. It is quite delicious.*

8 slices white sliced bread
vegetable oil for deep-
  frying
$1\frac{3}{4}$ pints (a good litre) milk
8 fl oz (250 ml) sweetened
  condensed milk
$\frac{1}{2}$ teaspoon saffron
a few drops of vanilla
  essence
$\frac{1}{2}$ teaspoon ground green
  cardamoms
a few drops of rosewater

Garnish
1 tablespoon almond flakes,
  roasted
1 tablespoon pistachio nuts,
  chopped
4 silver or gold leaf sheets
  (page 157)

1 Remove the crusts from the bread and discard. Deep-fry the bread at 375°F/190°C until golden. Remove and drain.

2 Using a non-stick pan (to prevent burning) bring the milk to the boil, then reduce the heat to a simmer. Add the condensed milk and simmer for 15 minutes to thicken it, stirring occasionally.

3 Add the saffron, vanilla essence and green cardamom, and take off the heat

4 Arrange four of the fried bread slices to cover the base of a small oven tray. Place the other slices on top. Pour the milk mixture over the bread, ensuring that the bread is thoroughly soaked.

5 Place the tray immediately into an oven preheated to 375°F/190°C/Gas 5. Bake for 15 minutes, then take out and cool. It will set firm.

6 When cold cut into four portions. Place on flat serving plates, and garnish with the nuts and the silver or gold leaf. Place in the fridge until ready to serve.

Serves: 4

KULFI
Indian Ice Cream

The concept of ice cream in India is by no means a modern one. Long before the advent of refrigerators and freezers kulfi was being made successfully. It probably started in its present form at the time of the Moghul emperors for it is known that every day a huge load of ice was despatched from the Punjabi hills to the emperors to ensure they always had chilled water, and no doubt kulfi, no matter where they were or whatever the temperature. (The emperors only drank water from the River Ganges, and it was collected and sent each day!)

This recipe from the **Gaylord Restaurant***, 79 Mortimer Street, London W1, requires the milk to be reduced – a lengthy process requiring very frequent stirring to prevent the milk burning. Traditionally kulfi is frozen in conical moulds – exactly the same shape as our ice cream cones. If you do not have this shape to hand use small yoghurt pots.*

> **9 pints (5 litres) full-cream milk (not UHT)**
> **9 oz (250 g) sugar**
> **$\frac{1}{2}$ teaspoon ground green cardamoms**
> **$2\frac{1}{2}$ oz (65 g) chopped nuts (almond, cashew and pistachio)**
> **a few drops of rosewater**

1 Using a wok, karahi or large saucepan – preferably with a non-stick surface – bring the milk to boiling point, then reduce the temperature to a simmer.

2 Stir frequently until the milk reduces to a thick consistency (like condensed milk) when it is called khoya. This is tedious and can take a very long time – an hour or more.

3 Remove from the stove and add the remaining ingredients (omit the nuts if you do not like that texture).

4 Place the mixture into kulfi moulds or yoghurt pots, and freeze.

5 On serving remove from the moulds, and garnish with more chopped nuts.

Makes: *10 kulfis*

MOIRA BANANA

In the state of Goa there is a town called Moira. It is not a place where tourists go, and it is unremarkable in many ways. But from that town I collected this deliciously simple recipe, which uses a particular kind of local banana. This is not exported, but I have found it works well with ordinary bananas.

2 tablespoons raisins

2 tablespoons sultanas

1 tablespoon chopped
    mixed nuts

2 tablespoons butter ghee

4 tablespoons brown sugar

2 tablespoons sherry or rum

4 large fresh bananas

1 Grind the raisins, sultanas and nuts in a food processor with a little water.

2 Heat the ghee with an equal quantity of water. Add the sugar and stir well. When simmering add the raisins, sultanas and nuts. Simmer for a while so that it thickens a little. Add the sherry or rum then take off the heat.

3 Peel and chop up the bananas. Pour the hot sauce over them and serve at once.

Serves: *4*

FRESH FRUIT SORBET

The word sorbet derives from sherbet, and is a frozen or water-ice version of the drink. Modern India has quickly learned the art of sorbet making, and it is a tasty way of enjoying exotic fruit, and goes especially well after the contrasting spicy tastes of curry. You can control the amount of sugar to achieve very tart or sweet tastes, whichever you prefer, and the fruit can be anything that is available. Fresh sorbets are available at the quaintly named **Tea Planters' Tiffin House**, *60 Western Road, Hove, Sussex.*

**12 oz (350 g) fruit, after de-
    skinning, seeding and
    puréeing**
**4 oz (100 g) granulated
    sugar**
10 fl oz (300 ml) water
juice of 1 lemon
1 egg white

1 Place the sugar and water in a saucepan and bring to the simmer. Continue simmering and stirring until the mixture becomes tacky.

2 Remove from the heat and allow to get cold.

3 Add the puréed fruit and the lemon juice. Mix well then freeze for exactly 1 hour.

4 Whip the egg white so that it is firm enough to form stiffish peaks. Fold into the cold fruit, and freeze again for at least 24 hours.

5 To serve, use an ice-cream scoop.

Serves: 4

APPENDIX 1

The Curry Club is all about curry. Whether your interest is cooking or dining out The Curry Club is dedicated to bringing you all you need to enhance your enjoyment of that extraordinary food.

Founded in January 1982 by Pat Chapman and Fiona Ross it now has many thousands of members throughout the UK and world-wide. Members receive a bright and colourful quarterly magazine which has regular features on curry and the curry lands. *The Curry Magazine* is produced on art paper and keeps members in touch with everything to do with curry. Original recipes appear, sometimes with photographs, from all countries which enjoy authentic curries – from India, Pakistan, Bangladesh, Nepal, Burma, Sri Lanka and further afield, from Singapore, Malaysia, Thailand, even China occasionally. Features about the history and culture of these fascinating lands back up the food side, and members regularly contribute by writing of their experiences. Readers' letters and members' reports on restaurants, 'Restaurant Roundup', are popular features. We write about spices and review curry cookery books and have some lighthearted pages with a crossword and puzzles, cartoons and sometimes stories and there's even a gossip column which keeps tabs on what the manufacturers and popular personalities are up to – and it's all curry, of course.

The Curry Club publishes *The Good Curry Guide*. It is a critical study of Indian-style restaurants throughout the country. Did you know there are over 3,000 Indian restaurants in the UK? Where are the best of these? The *Guide* lists and describes well over 1,000 plus a listing of overseas restaurants world-wide. It also contains features and background articles by well-known writers. We also operate a discount scheme for members at restaurants.

The Curry Club also runs a highly acclaimed and efficient mail order service. Over 200 items are stocked including whole spices, ground spices, pickles, pastes, dry foods, tinned food, joss sticks, gift packs and a full range of Indian cookbooks by other authors. We also offer a range of forty packs of pre-mixed spices which make dishes for four and, as well as removing the chore of mixing the spices, assists you in getting to know about them.

On the social side, the Club organises regular activities all over the UK. These range from a regular monthly club night in London and club nights from time to time elsewhere, enabling members to meet the Club organisers, discuss specific queries, buy supplies and enjoy curry snacks and meals, usually in the private function room of a pub or similar location. We also hold day and residential weekend cookery courses, gourmet nights to selected restaurants and similar enjoyable outings.

Top of the list is our regular Curry Club gourmet trip to India. We take a small group of curry enthusiasts, including ourselves, to India and tour the incredible sights all over the country in between sampling the foods of each region.

If you'd like to know more write to:
The Curry Club, PO Box 7, Haslemere, Surrey GU27 1EP.
Telephone: 0428 658 327.

APPENDIX 2

The Store Cupboard

There are well over sixty main spices and dried herbs in common use in Indian cookery. In addition there are over sixty pulse types, and dozens of rices, nuts and dry foods which you could use to cook Indian.

I've simplified this to a workable list of items you need in your store cupboard to make the recipes in this book, and of these, I have subdivided them into essential and non-essential. The essential items appear again and again in the recipes, the non-essential appear only in one or two.

Before you start cooking check your stores. Nothing guarantees putting you off a cookbook more than finding you don't have an ingredient. This list may look a bit formidable but remember once you have the items in stock they will last for some time. And again I have listed in metric only as most of the packaging these days *is* metric only.

All the items listed are available in the quantities stated, by post from The Curry Club.

ESSENTIAL WHOLE SPICES	**SUGGESTED QUANTITY**
Bay leaves	10 g
Cardamom, black or brown	50 g
Cardamom, green or white	50 g
Cassia bark	50 g
Chillies	50 g
Cloves	50 g
Coriander seeds	100 g
Cummin seeds, white	100 g
Curry leaves, dry	10 g

Fennel seeds	100 g
Fenugreek leaves, dry	50 g
Mustard seeds	100 g
Peppercorns, black	100 g
Sesame seeds	100 g
Wild onion seeds	100 g

ESSENTIAL GROUND SPICES

Black pepper	100 g
Chilli powder	100 g
Coriander	100 g
Cummin	100 g
Garam masala	100 g
Garlic powder	100 g
Ginger	100 g
Paprika	100 g
Turmeric	100 g

NON-ESSENTIAL
WHOLE SPICES

Alkenet root	25 g
Cinnamon bark	100 g
Cummin seeds, black	100 g
Dill seeds	100 g
Fenugreek seeds	100 g
Ginger, dried	100 g
Lovage seeds	100 g
Mace	100 g
Nutmeg, whole	50 g
Panch phoran	25 g
Pomegranate seeds	50 g
Poppy seeds	100 g
Saffron stamens	$\frac{1}{2}$ g

NON-ESSENTIAL
GROUND SPICES

Asafoetida	50 g
Cardamom, green	25 g
Cassia bark	25 g
Cloves	25 g
Mango powder	100 g

ESSENTIAL DRY FOODS

Basmati rice	2 kg
Desiccated coconut	100 g
Gram flour	1 kg
Masoor (red) lentils	500 g

NON-ESSENTIAL DRY FOODS

Bombay duck	200 g
Food colouring powder, red	25 g
Food colouring powder, yellow	25 g
Lentils – Channa, split	500 g
Moong green, whole	500 g
Toor or tovar, split	500 g
Urid, whole black	500 g
Nuts – Almond, whole	50 g
Almond, ground	100 g
Cashew	100 g
Peanuts, raw	100 g
Pistachio	100 g
Papadams, spiced and plain (pack)	300 g
Puffed rice (*mamra*)	500 g
Red kidney beans	500 g
Rice flour	500 g
Rosewater, bottle	7 fl oz
Sev (gram flour savoury)	200 g
Silver leaf (edible)	6 sheets
Supari mixture	100 g
Tamarind block	400 g

GLOSSARY

Included in this glossary is an explanation of some of the spices used in the recipes in this book. For a much more comprehensive glossary, please refer to the companion volume *The Curry Club Indian Restaurant Cookbook*.

A

Allspice Native to the West Indies. Related to the clove family, the seed resembles small dried peas. Called allspice because its aroma seems to combine those of clove, cinnamon, ginger, nutmeg and pepper. Used rather more in Middle Eastern cooking than Indian.

Am Chur Mango powder.

Aniseed Saunf. Small deliciously flavoured seeds resembling fennel seeds.

Asfoetida Hing. Gum obtained from root of giant fennel-like plant. Used in powder of resin form. A rather smelly spice.

Ata or Atta Chupatti flour. Fine wholemeal flour used in most Indian breads. English wholemeal is a suitable alternative.

B

Basmati The best type of long-grain rice.

Bay leaf This very well known leaf is used fresh or dried in certain Indian recipes.

Besan see gram flour

Blachan see Shrimp Paste

C

Cardamom Elaichi. One of the most aromatic and expensive spices. It is a pod containing slightly sticky black seeds.

There are three main types: *Brown* (also called black) have a rather hairy, husky, dark brown casing about 20 mm long. Used in garam masala, kormas and pullaos. Quite pungent *Green* have a smooth, pale green outer casing about 10 mm long. Used whole or ground, with or without casing in many savoury and sweet recipes. *White* are about the same size as green with a slightly rounder white casing. Green and white have a similar flavour – more delicate than the brown.

Cassia bark A corky bark with a sweet fragrance similar to cinnamon. Cassia is coarser and cooks better than cinnamon and is used extensively in northern Indian cookery. Although cooked in the curry, the bark is too coarse to eat.

Cayenne pepper A blend of chilli powder from Latin America.

Chana Type of lentil. See dhal.

Chilli There are a great many species of chillies, which are the fleshy pods of shrub-like bushes of the capsicum family. Chillies range from large to small, and colours include green, white, purple, pink and red. Curiously, although synonymous with Indian food they were only brought to the sub-continent from South America some four centuries ago. They are now the most important heat agent in Indian cookery. They vary in

hotness from mild to incendiary-like potency. Most commonly, small green or red chillies are used fresh. Red chillies can be dried and used whole, and chilli powder is made by grinding dried chillies.

Cinnamon Dalchini. The quill-like dried bark of the cinnamon tree. It is one of the most aromatic spices. Same family as cassia, it is generally used in dishes which require a delicate flavour.

Cloves Lavang. The most familiar spice in the UK where it has been continuously used since Roman times. Expensive and fragrant, it is an unopened flower bud.

Coriander Dhania. One of the most important spices in Indian cookery. The leaves of the plant can be used fresh and the seeds used whole or ground.

Cummin or Cumin Jeera. There are two types of seeds: *white* and *black*. The white seeds are a very important spice in Indian cookery. The black seeds (kala jeera) are nice in pullao rice and certain vegetable dishes. Both can be used whole or ground.

Curry The only word in this glossary to have no direct translation into any of the sub-continent's fifteen or so languages. The work was coined by the British in India centuries ago. Possible contenders for the origin of the word are, karahi or karai (Hindi), a wok-like frying-pan used all over India to prepare masalas (spice mixtures), karhi, a soup-like dish made with spices, gram flour dumplings and buttermilk, kair, a spicy Tamil sauce, Turkuri, a seasoned sauce or stew, or kari phulia, neem or curry leaves. Kudhi or kadhi, a yoghurt soup, or koresh, an aromatic Iranian stew.

Curry lands India is the main curry land with 600 million, mainly Hindu, people. Other curry lands are her Moslem neighbours to the west – Pakistan, Afghanistan, and, to a lesser extent, Iran which is the root of some Indian food. To the north lie Nepal and Bhutan whilst Moslem Bangladesh lies to the east. India's south-eastern curry-land neighbours include the predominantly Buddhist Burma and Thailand, whilst multinational Malaysia and Singapore, with huge, mainly Moslem Indian populations are also curry lands. The tiny island of Sri Lanka has a very distinctive curry style and one must not forget significant pockets of curry-eating Asians in Africa and the Caribbean. The total number of people whose 'staple' diet is curry exceeds 1 billion people – 25 per cent of the world's population.

Curry leaves Neem leaves or kari phulia. Small leaves a bit like bay leaves, used for flavouring.

D

Dhal Lentils. There are over sixty types of lentil in the sub-continent, some of which are very obscure. Like peas, they grow into a hard sphere measuring between 10 mm (chickpeas) and 3 mm (urid). They are cooked whole or split with skin, or split with it polished off. Lentils are a rich source of protein and when cooked with spices are extremely tasty. The common

types are chana (resembling yellow split peas, used to make gram flour/besam; kabli chana (chickpeas); masoor (the most familiar orangey-red lentil which has a green skin); moong (green skin lentil, used also to make beansprouts); toot, or toovar (dark yellow and very oily); and urid (black skin, white lentil).

Dhania Coriander.

F

Fennel Sonf or soonf. A small green seed which is very aromatic, with aniseed taste. Delicious in pullao rice.

Fenugreek Methi. This important spice is used as seeds and in fresh or dried leaf form. It is very savoury and is used in many Northern Indian dishes.

Fish sauce Nam-pla (Thai), Ngapya (Burmese), Patis (Philippine). It is the runny liquid strained from fermented anchovies, and is a very important flavouring agent.

Five Spice powder Combination of five sweet and aromatic spices used in Chinese and Malay cooking. Usually ground. A typical combination would be equal parts of cinnamon, cloves, fennel seeds, star anise and szechian pepper.

G

Galingale or Galangel A tuber related to ginger which comes in varieties called greater or lesser. It has a more peppery taste than ginger (which can be substituted for it). It is used in Thai cooking where it is called Kha, and in Indonesian (Laos) and Malay (Kenkur). It is available in the UK in fresh form (rare), dried or powdered.

Garam masala Literally 'hot mixture'. This refers to a blend of spices much loved in northern Indian cookery. Curry Club garam masala contains nine spices.

Ghee Clarified butter or margarine much used in northern Indian cookery.

Ginger Adrak (fresh), Sont (dried), a rhizome which can be used fresh, dried or powdered.

Gosht Lamb, mutton or goat.

Gram flour Besan. Finely ground flour, pale blonde in colour, made from chana (see Dhal). Used to make pakoras and to thicken curries.

H

Huldi Turmeric.

J

Jeera or Zeera Cummin.

K

Kabli chana Chickpeas. See Dhal.

Kalongi See wild onion seeds.

Karahi Karai, korai etc. Cast-iron, or steel wok-like frying or serving pan. Some restaurants cook in small karahis and serve them straight to the table with the food sizzling inside.

L

Lemon Grass Takrai (Thai), serai (Malay). A fragrant leafed plant which imparts a subtle lemony flavour to cooking. Use ground powder (made from the bulb) as a substitute.

Lentils see Dhal.

Lime Leaves Markrut or Citrus leaves. Used in Thai cooking – fresh or dried – to give a distinctive aromatic flavour.

Lovage Ajwain or ajowain. Slightly bitter round seeds.

M

Mango Powder Am Chur. A very sour flavouring agent.

Masala A mixture of spices which are cooked with a particular dish. Any curry powder is therefore a masala. It can be spelt a remarkable number of ways – massala, massalla, musala, mosola, massalam etc.

Masoor Red lentils. See Dhal.

Methi Fenugreek.

Mirch Pepper or chilli.

Moglai or Moghlai Cooking in the style of the Moghul emperors whose chefs took Indian cookery to the heights of gourmet cuisine three centuries ago. Few restaurateurs who offer Moglai dishes come anywhere near this excellence. True Moglai dishes are expensive and time-consuming to prepare authentically. Can also be variously spelt muglai, mhogulai, moghlai etc.

Moong Type of lentil. See Dahl.

Mustard seed Small black seeds which become sweetish when fried. Yellow variety used to make English mustard to which flour and colouring is added.

N

Nam Pla Fish sauce.

Nga-Pi Shrimp paste.

Nga-Pya Fish sauce.

Nigella Wild Onion Seed.

P

Papadam Thin lentil flour wafers. When cooked (deep fried or baked) they expand to about 8 inches (20 cm). They must be crackling crisp and warm when served. If not send them back to be re-heated and deduct points from that restaurant. They come plain or spiced with lentils, pepper, garlic or chilli. Many spelling variations include popodon, pappodon etc.

Paprika Mild red ground pepper made from red capsicum peppers. It originally came from Hungary and only reached India this century. Its main use is to give red colour to a dish.

Patna A long-grained rice.

Pepper Mirch. Has for centuries been India's most important spice, gaining it the title 'king of spices'. It grows on vines which flower triennially and produce clusters of berries, which are picked and dried and become the peppercorns. Green, black and white pepper are not different varieties. All peppercorns are green when picked and must be bottled or freeze-dried at once to retain the colour. Black pepper is the dried berry. White pepper is obtained by soaking off the black skin of the berry. Peppercorns are a heat agent and can be used whole or ground.

Pistachio nut Pista magaz. A fleshy, tasty nut which can be used fresh (the greener the better) or salted. It is expensive and goes well in savoury or sweet dishes such as biriani or pista kulfi (ice cream).

Poppy seed Cus cus. White seeds used to thicken curries; blue seeds used to decorate bread. Not to be confused with the Moroccan national dish – couscous – made from steamed semolina.

Pulses Types of lentils.

S

Saffron Kesar or zafron. The world's most expensive spice, saffron is the stigma of the crocus flower. A few stigmas are all that are needed to give a recipe a delicate yellow colouring and aroma.

Sesame seed Til. Small round discs, the white species are widely used in Indian cooking, the black in Chinese.

Shrimp paste Blachau (Malay), Nga-Pi (Burmese), Kapi (Thai). Very concentrated block of compressed shrimps. A vital flavourer for the cooking of those countries.

Star Anise A pretty star-shaped spice used in Chinese Five Spices, and it is lovely in pullao rice.

Sub-continent Term to describe India, Pakistan, Bangladesh, Nepal, Burma, and Sri Lanka as a group.

Supari Mixture of seeds and sweeteners for chewing after a meal. Usually includes aniseed or fennel, shredded betel nut, sugar balls, marrow seeds etc.

T

Tamarind Imli. A date-like fruit used as a chutney, and in cooking as a souring agent (see pages 42, 169).

Tej Patia The leaf of the cassia bark tree. Resembles bay leaf which can be used in its place.

Thali A tray which holds the complete meal served in individual bowls (katori). Used by diners in the south.

Toor or Toovar Type of lentil See Dahl.

Turmeric Haldi or huldi. A very important Indian spice, turmeric is a rhizome. The fresh root is used occasionally as a vegetable or in pickles. The ground spice is extensively used to give the familiar yellow colour to curries. Use sparingly or it can cause bitterness.

U

Urid A type of lentil. See Dahl.

V

Vark or Varak Edible silver or gold foil. See page 158.

W

Wild Onion Seed Kalongi. Small irregular jet-black nuggets which have an oniony fragrance though they are not from an onion species. Also known as Nigella.

INDEX